MW00973748

H. Richard Lamb, *University of Southern California*
EDITOR-IN-CHIEF

The Role of Organized Psychology in Treatment of the Seriously Mentally Ill

Frederick J. Frese, III
Northeast Ohio Universities
College of Medicine

EDITOR

**CONSUMER EDUCATIONAL
OUTREACH CENTER**
150 Cross St #316
Akron, OH 44311-1047
330-253-9388, ext. 316

Number 88, Winter 2000

JOSSEY-BASS
San Francisco

THE ROLE OF ORGANIZED PSYCHOLOGY IN TREATMENT
OF THE SERIOUSLY MENTALLY ILL
Frederick J. Frese, III (ed.)
New Directions for Mental Health Services, no. 88
H. Richard Lamb, Editor-in-Chief

Copyright ©2000 Jossey-Bass, a Wiley company.

All rights reserved. No part of this publication may be reproduced in any form or by any means, except as permitted under sections 107 and 108 of the 1976 United States Copyright Act, without either the prior written permission of the publisher or authorization through the Copyright Clearance Center, 222 Rosewood Drive, Danvers, MA 01923; (978) 750-8400; fax (978) 750-4470. The copyright notice appearing at the bottom of the first page of a chapter in this journal indicates the copyright holder's consent that copies may be made for personal or internal use, or for personal or internal use of specific clients, on the condition that the copier pay for copying beyond that permitted by law. This consent does not extend to other kinds of copying, such as copying for general distribution, for advertising or promotional purposes, for creating collective works, or for resale. Such permission requests and other permission inquiries should be addressed to the Permissions Department, John Wiley & Sons, Inc., 605 Third Avenue, New York, NY 10158-0012; (212) 850-6011, fax (212) 850-6008, e-mail: permreq@wiley.com.

Microfilm copies of issues and articles are available in 16mm and 35mm, as well as microfiche in 105mm, through University Microfilms Inc., 300 North Zeeb Road, Ann Arbor, Michigan 48106-1346.

ISSN 0193-9416   ISBN 0-7879-1437-1

NEW DIRECTIONS FOR MENTAL HEALTH SERVICES is part of The Jossey-Bass Psychology Series and is published quarterly by Jossey-Bass Inc., Publishers, 350 Sansome Street, San Francisco, California 94104-1342.

SUBSCRIPTIONS cost $66.00 for individuals and $121.00 for institutions, agencies, and libraries.

EDITORIAL CORRESPONDENCE should be sent to the Editor-in-Chief, H. Richard Lamb, University of Southern California, Department of Psychiatry, Graduate Hall, 1937 Hospital Place, Los Angeles, California 90033–1071.

Cover photograph by Wernher Krutein/PHOTOVAULT ©1990.

Jossey-Bass Web address: www.josseybass.com

Printed in the United States of America on acid-free recycled paper containing 100 percent recovered waste paper, of which at least 20 percent is postconsumer waste.

CONTENTS

Editor's Notes

Tremendous advances were made in the understanding and treatment of schizophrenia and other serious mental illnesses during the second half of the twentieth century. Beginning about fifty years ago, a revolution has been under way concerning how society views and treats mentally ill persons.

There have been major players in this revolution. Biologically oriented psychiatrists and their allies have made remarkable discoveries that have led to increasingly effective pharmacological treatments and fresh perspectives for viewing these disorders. Family members of victims of mental illness have forged effective advocacy efforts, pushing society to alter its posture concerning this population (Frese, 1998). And mental health lawyers and policymakers have been busy redirecting the social and political resources that have been available to address the various needs of mentally ill persons. As the new century unfolds, these three groups of dedicated individuals continue to be major players responsible for changing, and hopefully improving, conditions for mentally ill persons.

I am one of the persons who have benefited substantially from the pioneering efforts of these mental health activists. Having been diagnosed and hospitalized multiple times with schizophrenia beginning in the mid-1960s, I am most grateful for the work of those groups, which has allowed me to return to society and function in a dignified and professionally satisfying role. My adventures as a person with mental illness have been abundantly chronicled elsewhere in both the popular (Ansett, 1996; Spitz and Witek, 1994) and professional literature (Buie, 1989; Frese, 1993, 1994, 2000). Therefore, I will not repeat the many facts that so thoroughly establish my credentials as a consumer of psychiatric services.

However, I am also a psychologist who has spent virtually all my career working with and caring for persons with disorders similar to my own. During the twenty-five years that I worked in Ohio's state hospitals, as well as during my more recent tenure working in community mental health, I have been continually faced with an ongoing mystery about my own profession.

I see the consumers whom I work with as being severely psychologically disabled, and while I recognize that their disorders have biological underpinnings, it seems quite clear to me that the difficulties they have with their neurotransmitting systems clearly entail cognitive, behavioral, and perceptual correlates. In other words, there are serious psychological dimensions to these disorders that clearly should be addressed. Yet despite the critical need for attention to the psychological aspects of serious mental illness, organized psychology has yet to become a major player in the rapidly developing revolution that has been so markedly changing the lives of mentally ill persons.

New Directions for Mental Health Services, no. 88, Winter 2000   © Jossey-Bass

Recently a dramatic breakthrough occurred that may prove to be a strong indication that organized psychology's long-standing posture of benign neglect toward the mentally ill is starting to change. This event occurred at the annual convention of the American Psychological Association (APA) in August 1999. At that convention two of the members of the board of directors of the APA, Ronald Levant and Catherine Acuff, joined efforts with two of the authors in this issue, Ronald Bassman and Robert Coursey, and cochaired a special APA board of directors' mini-convention program. Entitled "Consumers and Psychologists in Dialogue," the program consisted of three days of continuous presentations, symposia, and a specially organized town hall meeting.

In the wake of that mini-convention, the APA published a cover article in its monthly *Monitor on Psychology* (2000) publication on schizophrenia. That same month in response to an invitation, the new APA president, Patrick DeLeon, met with the consumer and family advocates who make up the board of directors of the National Alliance for the Mentally Ill (NAMI). DeLeon gave assurances that organized psychology would increase its efforts to find common ground on which it could work more closely with advocates for the mentally ill.

All of these recent overtures of interest by leaders in the APA are harbingers of a more enthusiastic attention to the developing psychological needs of this vulnerable population.

Purpose of This Issue

This issue presents the work of some psychologists who have been making active contributions on behalf of persons with serious mental illness for extended periods of time.

The authors of the first two chapters are highly respected psychologists who have dedicated their careers to working with mentally ill persons in government-operated facilities. Richard Hunter lays out in Chapter One the rationale and recommendations for employing less controlling approaches to treatment. He weaves into his recommendations thinking based on sound psychological and behavioral principles.

In Chapter Two, Walter Penk reviews several programs that focus on the importance of work for persons with serious mental illnesses. He summarizes the activities he has been involved with and of programs in other locations where work initiatives for recovering persons are being developed.

The following three chapters are written by psychologists who have been forthright about having close family members with serious mental illness.

Dale Johnson explains in Chapter Three how he became personally involved in advocacy for the mentally ill. He also gives an overview of the activities of several organizations that are, or should be, advocating for improved conditions for mentally ill persons; describes several specific programs that he feels do a good job of serving this population; and argues for an approach to improving care that he believes family and consumer advocates can be particularly effective in implementing.

Harriet Lefley describes the interface between psychology and psychiatry in Chapter Four. She focuses on the possibility of prescription privileges being granted to psychologists and the implications for how this could alter incentives as to how members of this profession view service to this vulnerable population.

In Chapter Five, David Walling and Diane Marsh focus on the issue of relapse prevention, which they identify as a relatively new concept in this field. Using the vulnerability-stress model as a framework, the authors lay out symptom triggers, risk, and protective factors. They then discuss implications for psychoeducation, psychotherapy, lifestyle management, and various other approaches to these problems. Finally, they discuss practical opportunities for psychologists to become more involved in helping the mentally ill by attending to various aspects of relapse prevention.

Robert Coursey and Carol Mowbray, the lead authors of the following two chapters, have spent their careers in academia, where they have demonstrated long-term interest in persons with serious mental illness. Each has invited associates to coauthor their chapters. Robert Coursey and his coauthors rely heavily on first-person accounts in integrating consumers' views with psychological concepts in Chapter Six. The authors draw from their previous work in blending a competency framework with an Acceptance of Disability model and gender considerations to construct a model for better understanding of mentally ill persons.

Carol Mowbray, Daphna Oyserman, and Deborah Bybee give in Chapter Seven an overview of a report on what they describe as "the largest longitudinal study undertaken of mothering among women with mental illness, recruited from the public sector." They point out the great need for more professional attention to this population and stress the value of psychological approaches to meeting the needs of these disabled women and their families.

The final chapters are written by persons who are psychologists and, like myself, have been diagnosed and hospitalized for schizophrenia. Ronald Bassman describes in Chapter Eight some of his experiences as a recipient of psychiatric treatment. He then relates how he draws on these experiences and those of other consumers/survivors/ex-patients to help train staff members working in state-operated mental health facilities.

Al Siebert, who kept his experiences as a recipient of psychiatric services a secret for some thirty years, now relates in detail in Chapter Nine how he came to be treated for schizophrenia, a condition that he seriously questions that he ever had. Based in large part on his interactions with various mental health personnel, Siebert makes recommendations as to how treatment for persons with serious mental illness might be improved.

Taken as a whole, this issue presents a wide spectrum of viewpoints from psychologists who have dedicated their professional careers to striving for a better quality of life for persons with serious mental illnesses. Thanks in part to the efforts of these pioneering practitioners, those who have too often been abandoned and even ostracized by mainstream psychology and the other mental health professions will begin to find compassionate and effective services for their long-neglected needs.

Frederick J. Frese, III
Editor

References

Ansett, P. "Living with Schizophrenia." *Detroit Free Press*, June 18, 1996, pp. 8F-10F.

Buie, J. "Psychologist Prevails Despite Schizophrenia." *APA Monitor*, 1989, *20*(5), 23.

Frese, F. J. "Cruising the Cosmos, Part Three: Psychosis and Hospitalization. A Consumer's Personal Recollection." In A. B. Hatfield and H. P. Lefley (eds.), *Surviving Mental Illness: Stress, Coping, and Adaptation.* New York: Guilford Press, 1993.

Frese, F. J. "A Calling." *Second Opinion*, 1994, *19*(3), 11–25.

Frese, F. J. "Advocacy, Recovery, and the Challenges of Consumerism for Schizophrenia." In P. Buckley (ed.), *Psychiatric Clinics of North America.* Philadelphia: Saunders, 1998.

Frese, F. J. "Psychology Practitioners and Schizophrenia: A View from Both Sides." *Journal of Clinical Psychology/In Session: Psychotherapy in Practice*, 2000, *56*(11), 1–14.

Spitz, K., and Witek, R. "The Odyssey of Fred Frese." *Beacon, (Magazine of the Akron Beacon Journal)*, Mar. 6, 1994, pp. 1–13.

FREDERICK J. FRESE, III is an assistant professor of psychology in psychiatry at the Northeast Ohio Universities College of Medicine and is serving as the first vice president of the National Alliance for the Mentally Ill.

1

Outcomes in psychiatric care are improved by expanding treatment options and reducing dependence on management and control interventions.

Treatment, Management, and Control: Improving Outcomes Through More Treatment and Less Control

Richard H. Hunter

Research over the past several years has increasingly demonstrated the value of psychosocial treatment interventions (those resulting in permanent skill enhancement) (Dilk and Bond, 1996; Heinssen, Liberman, and Kopelowicz, 2000; Penn and Mueser, 1996), yet over that same period, services offered to people with psychosis and other major mental disorders have lacked access to these interventions (Lehman, Steinwachs, and the Coinvestigators of the PORT Project, 1998; Lehman, 2000) or, in many cases, psychosocial interventions have been reduced or eliminated in favor of management (primarily medications) and control interventions (Hunter, 1999). Thus, coercive interventions have increased for that subset of people who refuse or otherwise do not benefit significantly from medications, resulting in less favorable outcomes. Cognitive deficits are the major factor producing functional disability in schizophrenia after the acute phase of the illness (Silverstein, 1999), and the failure to invest in behavioral, psychological, psychosocial, and rehabilitation interventions is leaving people overly dependent on medication to manage symptoms. Moreover, by not attending to cognitive deficits and the direct treatment of behavior disorders in a meaningful way, people with psychosis and other significant mental illnesses are subjected to a lifetime of unnecessary suffering, conflict, and increased risk of hospitalization, incarceration, and homelessness. This chapter discusses the value of treatment and rehabilitation of psychosis and behavior disorders and provides an example of how psychological case formulation strategies can lead to improved (less coercive) care and treatment.

NEW DIRECTIONS FOR MENTAL HEALTH SERVICES, no. 88, Winter 2000 © Jossey-Bass

A Framework for Categorizing Interventions

Categorizing interventions as treatment, management, and control allows us to describe varying levels of interventions more precisely, evaluate the comprehensiveness of a plan of care, and more readily understand the value of various intervention techniques (Gardner and Cole, 1987; Gardner and Hunter, 1995). All three types of interventions are appropriate given certain circumstances.

Treatment involves interventions that lead to permanent change in an individual. Competency-based interventions (Hunter, 1995; Hunter and Marsh, 1994; Bedell, Hunter, and Corrigan, 1997) and psychotherapy are examples of treatment interventions. After treatment, the person has a new understanding, additional skills, increased coping mechanisms, or enhanced immunities to the vicissitudes of his or her illness.

Management procedures are those that aid in the reduction of symptoms, but when the procedure is stopped, the person is at equal risk of relapse. No permanent change can be identified. Psychiatric medications are the best examples of management techniques. Other procedures, such as deep-breathing instructions and nonexclusionary time-out, are examples of other management techniques.

Control interventions are those that suppress the person's ability to respond. Examples are the sedative effects of antipsychotic medications when used to control behavior, seclusion, and physical restraints.

Designing Comprehensive Interventions

The importance of distinguishing among treatment, management, and control techniques is evident when examining outcomes of various programs. Programs that include competency-based (treatment) protocols, coupled with appropriate use of medications (management), have demonstrated better outcomes than alternatives (Bedell, Hunter, and Corrigan, 1997; Benton and Schroeder, 1990; Bachrach, 1992; Bellack, Turner, Hersen, and Luber, 1984; Brenner, Boker, Hodel, and Wyss, 1989; Corrigan, 1991; Coursey, Alford, and Safarjan, 1997; Liberman and others, 1998), improved community functioning, and decreased relapse rates (Liberman, Mueser, and Wallace, 1986; Wallace and Liberman, 1985; Stein and Test, 1980; Olfson, 1990; Leff and others, 1990; Hogarty and others, 1979, 1986, 1991). Furthermore, other studies have reported a lessening dependence on medications to manage symptoms as skills-based interventions have been provided (Liberman and others, 1994, 1998; Falloon and others, 1985; Hunter, 1995; Paul and Lentz, 1977). Programs that use an appropriate mix of treatment and management interventions obtain the best outcomes. Control interventions are used only in rare instances when there is immediate and imminent risk of harm to the person or others and it has been demonstrated that less restrictive alternatives would not avert the emergency.

In testimony before the Joint Commission on Accreditation of Health-care Organizations's public hearings on seclusion and restraint, Hunter (1999, pp. 3–4) stated:

> Having visited a variety of facilities over the years in a consulting capacity, the author has observed an alarming trend in how aggression and violence, along with other behavior disorders, are managed in inpatient settings. As psychiatric hospitals, both public and private, experienced economic challenges, downsizing, and service cutbacks, there has been a reduction in the availability and sophistication of psychological and behavioral interventions, a move away from studying and treating the functional properties of behavior disorders, and an increase in the use of high dosages of psychoactive medications leading in many instances to chemical restraints. Further, the absence of sophisticated psychological and behavioral interventions focusing on the direct treatment of behavior dysfunction has led to the continuation of ineffective medication strategies and the unnecessary use of restraints and seclusion. Reducing this often unnecessary and inappropriate application of restrictive practices requires staff to take responsibility for the direct treatment of behavior disorders, including acts of aggression and violence by patients under their care.

A variety of influences have an impact on the service system. Overdependence on biochemical theories of mental disorders, a society oriented to quick-fix medical and chemical solutions to complex problems, and beliefs influenced by the massive promotion of drugs by the pharmaceutical industry (Valenstein, 1998 and Glenmullen, 2000), coupled with stringent health care cost containment strategies, have forced many public and private mental health systems into providing the least expensive treatment possible. Lauriello, Bustillo, and Keith (2000, p. 141) note "managed care's increasing pressures to treat all patients as 'med checks.'" Far too often this strategy has left people who have serious and complex illnesses a restricted array of services that has been described as "drugs and TV therapy" (Hunter, 1999). Reviews of treatment-refractory cases and clinical records of patients with behavioral disorders often reveal that the primary, and often the only, meaningful intervention a person with serious mental illness receives while in public or private psychiatric hospitals today is psychoactive medications. Drugs are an important component for most people with major mental illnesses. However, the best medications in psychiatry only manage symptoms; they do not treat the illness or cause permanent changes in the person's neural functioning. Medications are frequently necessary to manage symptoms or in rare situations as a control (restraint) mechanism for dangerous behaviors. When psychological and behavioral interventions are developed to treat behavior dysfunction directly, the use of high dosages of psychoactive drugs is reduced or eliminated.

Further distinction can be made between management and control when describing the effects of psychotropic medications. When the medications are provided as a means of managing acute symptoms (such as reducing hallucinations, delusions, or other positive symptoms of the illness), the intervention is categorized as a management intervention. If the medications are used primarily for behavior control (such as sedation), they are categorized as a control intervention and often referred to as chemical restraint. Clinicians who use medications as the primary form of interventions and do not provide focused psychological, behavioral, psychosocial, and rehabilitation interventions for behavior dysfunction are at a loss when behavior escalates and aggression or violence emerges. Their limited case formulation and intervention strategies, driven by the belief that there is a chemical solution to every problem, leave them with few options other than to try more drugs or implement coercive and controlling interventions. Often this leads to more distress on the part of the clients, which exacerbates their problems even more.

As public service programs have deteriorated (Torrey, Wolfe, and Flynn, 1988; Torrey, Erdman, Wolfe, and Flynn, 1990) and as managed cost programs have put increased pressure on the funding for services over the years, many providers have eliminated psychological, behavioral, and psychosocial interventions and filled the void with the overuse and misuse of medications to manage or control symptoms and maladaptive behaviors. High relapse rates, increases in adverse side effects of drugs, increased use of restrictive and coercive programming, inappropriate use of seclusion and restraints, client and family dissatisfaction, and increased suffering are often the result (Hunter, 1995).

Despite significant advances in pharmacological research, many people remain refractory to biochemical interventions. Liberman and others (1998, p. 182) stated:

> Despite the advent of Clozapine, many thousands of patients with schizophrenia remain refractory to pharmacotherapy and customary forms of psychosocial treatment. Estimates of treatment refractoriness approximate 25% of persons with schizophrenia, a problem of public mental health magnitude, given the residence of these individuals in state hospitals, community facilities, prisons, and on the streets.

Torrey (1995, p. 192) reports "that approximately 70 percent of patients with schizophrenia clearly improve on these drugs, 25 percent improve minimally or not at all, and 5 percent get worse." Thirty percent with minimal or no substantive positive response results in large numbers of people with unmet needs and poor outcomes when programs are restricted to management and control techniques.

Most people admitted to public psychiatric hospitals and the vast majority of people involuntarily admitted for psychiatric care, in public or private hospitals, have exhibited a variety of behavior problems in addition to the symptoms of their diagnosed mental illnesses. These psychological and behavior problems often are not treated. Furthermore, most of these individuals have experienced years of various medication regimens with marginal, if any, effect. To incarcerate them involuntarily in a residential environment where they will only receive additional biochemical interventions that have proven to be ineffective in the past, while not attending to the direct treatment of the accompanying behavioral disorders and instrumental and social skills deficits at a minimum, amounts to neglect. Yet in clinical case reviews this approach is found repeatedly (Hunter, 1999).

The addition of treatment programs with psychological, social, and educational interventions is critical to improving the quality of life of people with serious mental illness (Bedell, Hunter, and Corrigan, 1997; Hunter, 1995; Liberman, Kopelowicz, and Smith, 1999; Liberman and others, 1998). Understanding how treatment, management, and control interventions differ improves clinicians' ability to plan effectively and implement comprehensive services; implement psychological, behavioral, and psychosocial interventions that lead to increased understanding and control on the part of the clients; decrease aggression and violence in psychiatric settings; improve client outcomes; and effectively invite the meaningful participation of clients into the treatment process (Heinssen, Levendusky, and Hunter, 1995; Heinssen and Hunter, 1998).

Comprehensive services require attention to both treatment and rehabilitation. For many clients, treatment must be developed for both the symptoms of the mental illness and any co-occurring behavior dysfunction (see Exhibit 1.1). Ensuring that plans of care include the direct treatment and rehabilitation of behavior dysfunction, in addition to the treatment and management of the symptoms of the mental illness, is critical to improved outcomes.

Case Illustration

Mr. Walters was a thirty-eight-year-old single male diagnosed with paranoid schizophrenia.[1] He resided in a state psychiatric hospital that served a forensic population. The treatment team invited me to review Mr. Walter's case after he had been returned from his fourth unauthorized absence over a five-year period. These "escapes" were causing the facility embarrassment since Mr. Walters had previously been charged with a high-profile crime, and the local press was critical of the facility for not providing adequate security.

When I met with the treatment team, the following story emerged. Mr. Walters suffered from paranoid schizophrenia beginning in his early twenties. He reported bothersome hallucinations and delusions and was only minimally responsive to the wide range of antipsychotic medications attempted over the previous seventeen years. At the time of this review, Mr. Walters was taking the maximum permitted dosage of the antipsychotic

**Exhibit 1.1. Components of Comprehensive Treatment
and Rehabilitation**

I. Treatment
   A. Acute symptoms of the mental illness
   B. Behavior dysfunction
II. Rehabilitation
   A. Social functioning
      1. Family
      2. Friends
      3. Leisure
      4. Social role performance
   B. Instrumental functioning
      1. Medication management
      2. Health and symptom management
      3. Stress management
      4. Money management
      5. Food preparation
      6. Vocational skills
      7. Time management
      8. Personal hygiene
      9. Care of possessions
      10. Housing
      11. Transportation
      12. Safety
   C. Consumer and family psychoeducation
III. Linkage and Community Support
   A. Housing
   B. Medical/dental care
   C. Transportation
   D. Program for Assertive Community Treatment follow-up

medication haloperidol, coupled with a substantial dosage of carbamazepine. Over the years, he had received numerous antipsychotic medications, including clozapine and various other combinations of antipsychotic medications with benzodiazepines and anticonvulsants. His responses to these medications were marginal at best. He exhibited multiple signs of adverse reactions, including parkinsonism, dystonia, and tardive dyskinesia.

Over the course of the previous five years, Mr. Walters had experienced frequent and extended periods of ward confinement, loss of privileges, physical restraints, and loss of telephone privileges. His attendance at off-unit programs was sporadic due to his various restrictions. Furthermore, his high medication regimens and the effects of these drugs on his cognitive and motor abilities inhibited his participation in psychosocial rehabilitation programming.

I was invited to participate in the team staffing following Mr. Walters's latest unauthorized absence. It was obvious that staff members were perplexed over his recent escape and the pressure they felt to control his behavior. However, they did not consider the functional properties of this behavior in suggesting solutions. The team members, well-trained and experienced clinicians, concentrated on further restrictions and repeatedly pressured the psychiatrist to add or otherwise alter medications. Requests were made to increase the antipsychotic medication above even the already high dosages. Staff disregarded seventeen years of evidence that increasing dosages and combinations of antipsychotic drugs had never eliminated his "running" behavior in the past, and they overlooked the obvious damaging neurological effects the drugs were having on Mr. Walters. Staff pleaded with the psychiatrist to add a benzodiazepine, change to another antipsychotic medication, or increase the carbamazapine. This pressure on the psychiatrist to do something with drugs permeated the entire team, although there were psychologists present who could have suggested a more focused approach to treating or managing the behavior.

In addition to altering medication regimens, the team vigorously debated additional physical restrictions for Mr. Walters. Some wanted another three-month restriction to the unit with no off-unit programs permitted. Others wanted off-unit programs to continue but to require one-to-one staff escort at all times. Others wanted Mr. Walters secluded for several days as a punishment for his escape. This lengthy discussion of restrictive interventions continued until I initiated a new line of questioning and case formulation.

I encouraged the staff to rethink this case and expand its case formulation strategies to include information about the antecedent conditions related to the escape behavior. Staff had unconsciously assumed that Mr. Walters ran because he was "paranoid and psychotic." Assuming therefore that this state automatically means a person will want to escape and the primary treatment of paranoid schizophrenia is medications, they felt it appropriate to keep adding medications and restrictions. Staff were reminded that this limited case formulation approach had not worked for the past five years, so what evidence did they have that it would work now? With some reluctance, the staff agreed to begin a functional assessment process in order to learn more about the meaning of the target behavior and its specific antecedents.

Mr. Walters was interviewed, and with further joint staff and client deliberations, the following scenario emerged. Mr. Walters had suffered for many years with hallucinations and delusions associated with his diagnosis of paranoid schizophrenia. Antipsychotic medications at minimal dosages had effectively relieved his tormenting hallucinations but had no effect on his delusional system. Increasing dosages brought no further improvements in the management of his acute symptoms.

Prior to hospitalization, he had lived alone with his dog, his most favored companion. When he was arrested, he had asked his mother to take his dog in. But he knew his mother did not like his dog, and since his initial incarceration he had worried that she would not care for the dog properly and that something "is likely to happen to him." He was also worried about his mother's health, and for good reason. She had major health complications and was becoming increasingly dependent on care herself.

The hospital provided one twenty-minute call per week for clients to contact families. The procedure required the person to call the hospital switchboard operator, who then dialed the number. After the parties had been talking for twenty minutes, the operator would come on the line and notify the client that the call must be ended. Mr. Walters reported that when he made these calls to his mother, she always became upset with him. Because of his delusional system, Mr. Walters concluded that the operator was changing his words in order to upset his mother and filtering and changing her replies in a way to hurt him. He maintained this delusion and was reluctant to make calls on the hospital telephone system. It was revealing that on each of his previous escapes from the hospital, he was located in or around a strip mall approximately two miles from the hospital. He had been picked up at a pay phone, in a grocery store, and in a pizza restaurant, all in the same mall. The staff were asked to think about why that might happen. Would a person wanting to escape repeatedly go to the same location, only to be easily found? Mr. Walters simply wanted to contact his mother using a "clean" telephone. He would risk the consequences of restraints and lengthy restrictions in order to check on the welfare of his mother and his dog.

As a result of this information, staff generated new clinical hypotheses that directed more focused interventions related to his behavior. Mr. Walters was asked to assist in the design of a therapeutic treatment contract that would provide him access to an outside telephone. Because contact with his mother was a valued objective and since no amount of medication would affect his delusional system, it was decided to begin lowering his medications and removing the expressed need for escape by providing him weekly access to an outside pay phone. Over time, the following treatment contract emerged. Every Friday afternoon staff would escort Mr. Walters to the pay phone in the strip mall so he could place a call to his mother. Medication was lowered to a minimal dosage of haloperidol, a level that controlled his hallucinations but did not lead to sedation or complicate his neurological symptoms. Eventually all other remaining medications were eliminated. He was allowed to participate in off-unit psychosocial programs; however, a one-to-one escort was maintained for an extended period. With the reduction of medication, his alertness and cognitive abilities improved to the point where his meaningful participation in his programs was possible.

Mr. Walters indicated he particularly enjoyed eating pizza at the strip mall and strolling through the grocery store. His treatment contract gave him an extra hour each Friday to visit the strip mall after his phone call on weeks when his attendance and participation in off-unit programs exceeded a 70 percent criterion.

In a few months Mr. Walters became a model patient. He enjoyed his programs and became a group leader in a unit socialization group. He earned the trust of the staff, obtained the freedom to walk unescorted to off-unit programs, and obtained a campus pass; a volunteer was recruited to escort Mr. Walters on his Friday town pass. His life at the hospital was totally changed, and his relationship with staff and peers became therapeutic.

The major changes leading to Mr. Walters's success involved staff, not Mr. Walters himself. When staff expanded their case formulation strategies, they were in a better position to understand the underlying causes and meaning of the aberrant behavior and to develop specific treatment interventions that were focused on the hypothesized antecedents. These interventions were far more effective than the management and control interventions (drugs, restrictions, and restraints) that had permeated their practice. Mr. Walters finally received the assistance he deserved, and his quality of life in that hospital improved dramatically.

Note

1. This case represents a truncated and blended case report.

References

Bachrach, L. L. "Psychosocial Rehabilitation and Psychiatry in the Care of Long-Term Patients." *American Journal of Psychiatry*, 1992, *149*, 1455–1463.

Bedell, J. R., Hunter, R. H., and Corrigan, P. W. "Current Approaches to Assessment and Treatment of Persons with Serious Mental Illness." *Professional Psychology: Research and Practice*, 1997, *3*, 217–228.

Bellack, A. S., Turner, S. M., Hersen, M., and Luber, R. F. "An Examination of the Efficacy of Social Skills Training for Chronic Schizophrenic Patients." *Hospital and Community Psychiatry*, 1984, *35*, 1023–1028.

Benton, M. K., and Schroeder, H. E. "Social Skills Training with Schizophrenics: A Meta-Analytic Evaluation." *Journal of Consulting and Clinical Psychology*, 1990, *58*, 741–747.

Brenner, H. D., Boker, W., Hodel, B., and Wyss, H. "Cognitive Treatment of Basic Pervasive Dysfunctions in Schizophrenia." In S. C. Schultz and C. A. Tamminga (eds.), *Schizophrenia: Scientific Progress*. New York: Oxford University Press, 1989.

Corrigan, P. W. "Social Skills Training in Adult Psychiatric Populations: A Meta-Analysis." *Journal of Behavior Therapy and Experimental Psychology*, 1991, *22*, 203–210.

Coursey, R. D., Alford, J., and Safarjan, W. "Significant Advances in Understanding and Treating Serious Mental Illness." *Professional Psychology: Research and Practice*, 1997, *28*, 205–216.

Dilk, M. N., and Bond, G. R. "Meta-Analytic Evaluation of Skills Training Research for Individuals with Severe Mental Illness." *Journal of Consulting and Clinical Psychology*, 1996, *64*, 1337–1346.

Falloon, I.R.H., and others. "Family Management in the Prevention of Morbidity of Schizophrenia: Clinical Outcome of a Two-Year Longitudinal Study." *Archives of General Psychiatry*, 1985, *42*, 887–896.

Gardner, W. I., and Cole, C. L. "Behavior Treatment, Behavior Management, and Behavior Control: Needed Distinctions." *Behavioral Residential Treatment*, 1987, *2*, 37–53.

Gardner, W. I., and Hunter, R. H. "The Multimodal Functional Model Enhances Treatment for People with Serious Mental Illness." Unpublished manuscript, 1995.

Glenmullen, J. *Prozac Backlash: Overcoming the Dangers of Prozac, Zoloft, Paxil, and Other Antidepressants with Safe, Effective Alternatives.* New York: Simon & Schuster, 2000.

Heinssen, R. K., and Hunter, R. H. "Therapeutic Contracting: An Effective Strategy for Competency-Based Treatment." *Psychiatric Rehabilitation Skills*, 1998, 2(2), 128–148.

Heinssen, R. K., Levendusky, P. G., and Hunter, R. H. "Client as Colleague: Therapeutic Contracting with the Seriously Mentally Ill." *American Psychologist*, 1995, 50(7), 522–532.

Heinssen, R. K., Liberman, R. P., and Kopelowicz, A. "Psychosocial Skills Training for Schizophrenia: Lessons from the Laboratory." *Schizophrenia Bulletin*, 2000, 26(1), 21–46.

Hogarty, G. E., and others. "Fluphenazine and Social Therapy in the Aftercare of Schizophrenic Patients." *Archives of General Psychiatry*, 1979, 36, 1283–1294.

Hogarty, G. E., and others. "Family Psychoeducation, Social Skills Training, and Maintenance Chemotherapy in Aftercare Treatment of Schizophrenia. I: One-Year Effects of a Controlled Study on Relapse and Expressed Emotion." *Archives of General Psychiatry*, 1986, 43, 633–642.

Hogarty, G. E., and others. "Family Psychoeducation, Social Skills Training, and Maintenance Chemotherapy in the Aftercare Treatment of Schizophrenia. II: Two-Year Effects of a Controlled Study on Relapse and Adjustment." *Archives of General Psychiatry*, 1991, 48, 340–347.

Hunter, R. H. "Benefits of Competency-Based Treatment Programs." *American Psychologist*, 1995, 50, 509–513.

Hunter, R. H. Testimony on behalf of the American Psychological Association at the Joint Commission on Accreditation of Healthcare Organizations (JCAHO) Public Hearings on the Use of Seclusion and Restraint in Psychiatric Facilities, Apr. 13, 1999. Alexandria, Va.

Hunter, R. H., and Marsh, D. T. "Mining Giftedness: A Challenge for Psychologists." In D. T. Marsh (ed.), *New Directions in the Psychological Treatment of Serious Mental Illness.* New York: Praeger, 1994.

Lauriello, J., Bustillo, J., and Keith, S. J. "Commentary: Can Intensive Psychosocial Treatments Make a Difference in a Time of Atypical Antipsychotics and Managed Care?" *Schizophrenia Bulletin*, 2000, 26(1), 141–144.

Leff, J., and others. "A Trial of Family Therapy Versus a Relatives' Group for Schizophrenia: Two-Year Follow-up." *British Journal of Psychiatry*, 1990, 157, 571–577.

Lehman, A. F. "Commentary: What Happens to Psychosocial Treatments on the Way to the Clinic?" *Schizophrenia Bulletin*, 2000, 26, 137–139.

Lehman, A. F., Steinwachs, D. M., and the Coinvestigators of the PORT Project. "Translating Research into Practice: The Schizophrenia Patient Outcomes Research Team (PORT) Treatment Recommendations." *Schizophrenia Bulletin*, 1998, 24, 1–10.

Liberman, R. P., Kopelowicz, A., and Smith, T. E. "Psychiatric Rehabilitation." In B. J. Sadock and V. A. Sadock (eds.), *Comprehensive Textbook of Psychiatry.* (7th ed.) Hagerstown, Md.: Lippincott Williams and Wilkins, 1999.

Liberman, R. P., Mueser, K. T., and Wallace, C. J. "Social Skills Training for Schizophrenic Individuals at Risk for Relapse." *American Journal of Psychiatry*, 1986, 143, 523–526.

Liberman, R. P., and others. "Optimal Drug and Behavior Therapy for Treatment-Refractory Schizophrenic Patients." *American Journal of Psychiatry*, 1994, 151, 756–759.

Liberman, R. P., and others. "Biobehavioral Therapy: Interactions Between Pharmacotherapy and Behavior Therapy in Schizophrenia." In T. Wykes, N. Tarrier, and S. Lewis (eds.), *Outcome and Innovation in Psychological Treatment of Schizophrenia.* New York: Wiley, 1998.

Olfson, M. "Assertive Community Treatment: An Evaluation of the Experimental Evidence." *Hospital and Community Psychiatry*, 1990, 41, 634–641.

Paul, G. L., and Lentz, R. J. *Psychosocial Treatment of Chronic Mental Patients: Milieu Versus Social-Learning Programs.* Cambridge, Mass.: Harvard University Press, 1977.

Penn, D. L., and Mueser, K. T. "Research Update on the Psychosocial Treatment of Schizophrenia." *American Journal of Psychiatry,* 1996, *153,* 607–617.

Silverstein, S. "Introduction to Special Issue: Cognitive Rehabilitation." *Psychiatric Rehabilitation Skills,* 1999, *3*(1), 21–22.

Stein, L. I., and Test, M. A. "Alternative to Mental Hospital Treatment. I: Conceptual Model, Treatment Program, and Clinical Evaluation." *Archives of General Psychiatry,* 1980, *37,* 392–397.

Torrey, E. F. *Surviving Schizophrenia: A Manual for Families, Consumers and Providers.* (3rd ed.) New York: HarperCollins, 1995.

Torrey, E. F., Erdman, K., Wolfe, S. M., and Flynn, L. M. *Care of the Seriously Mentally Ill: A Rating of State Programs.* (3rd ed.) Washington, D.C.: Public Citizen Health Research Group and the National Alliance for the Mentally Ill, 1990.

Torrey, E. F., Wolfe, S. M., and Flynn, L. M. *Care of the Seriously Mentally Ill: A Rating of State Programs.* (2nd ed.) Washington, D.C.: Public Citizen Health Research Group and the National Alliance for the Mentally Ill, 1988.

Valenstein, E. S. *Blaming the Brain: The Truth About Drugs and Mental Health.* New York: Free Press, 1998.

Wallace, C. J., and Liberman, R. P. "Social Skills Training for Patients with Schizophrenia: A Controlled Clinical Trial." *Psychiatry Research,* 1985, *15,* 239–247.

RICHARD H. HUNTER is president and founder of the consulting firm Clinical Outcomes Group, a clinical associate professor in the Department of Psychiatry, Southern Illinois University School of Medicine, and a member of the American Psychological Association Task Force on Serious Mental Illness.

2

Persons with serious mental disorders need to participate in productive activities, including mainstream, competitive employment, during the course of their treatment and recovery.

Designing Work Experiences for Persons with Serious Mental Disorders

Walter Erich Penk

No other technique for the conduct of life attaches the individual so firmly to reality as laying emphasis on work; for work at least gives one a secure place in a portion of reality, in the human community.

Sigmund Freud, *Civilization and Its Discontents*

Most psychiatric diagnoses identify interferences in occupational adjustment as one of several criteria for defining mental disorders. For example, the *Diagnostic and Statistical Manual of Mental Disorders* (4th edition) DSM-IV lists "social/occupational dysfunction" as the second of three sets of criteria for classifying schizophrenia. Schizophrenia is classified in part when, "since the onset of the disturbance, one or more major areas of functioning such as work, interpersonal relations, or self-care are markedly below the level achieved prior to onset."

Unfortunately, when treating serious mental disorders or evaluating outcomes of treatment, clinicians and researchers limit their attention to the first set of criteria, like hallucinations and delusions. Rarely do they either evaluate or examine the occupational dysfunctional features of a disorder as outcomes in the course of diagnosing or treating such disorders. And virtually none of the clinical trials for new medications in the treatment of schizophrenia tests outcomes in terms of unemployment, even though unemployment is one criterion in diagnosing schizophrenia.

As surveys of the past have shown, severe interferences in vocational adjustment remain long after other symptoms of mental disorders are in remission (Spaniol, Gagne, and Koehler, 1997). Surveys conducted at the Center for Psychiatric Rehabilitation at Boston University report unemployment rates as high as 90 percent once a person receives a diagnosis of schizophrenia.

Although rates of unemployment among persons with serious mental disorders are decreasing, nevertheless they remain unacceptably high, in spite of the fact that psychologists are finding that vocational rehabilitation can reduce interferences in productive activities and in employment. Unemployment can be reduced if psychologists form collaborative relationships with persons in recovery, where the goals of such partnerships are to find working environments tailored to the needs and choices of these persons (Danley and Anthony, 1987).

The major new direction in rehabilitation is the shift from a custodial rationale to a rehabilitation rationale. A rehabilitation rationale is based on the assumption that persons in recovery can and will return to work and learn new skills for choosing, getting, and keeping new jobs (Anthony, Cohen, and Danley, 1988; Anthony, Rogers, Cohen, and Davies, 1995; Cook and Solomon, 1993; Drake, Mercer-McFadden, Mueser, McHugo, and Bond, 1998).

Clinicians are reporting new forms of work environments and new approaches to mainstream employment for persons with serious mental disorders (National Institute on Disability and Rehabilitation Research, 1992; International Association of Psychosocial Rehabilitation Services, 1994). These new approaches are associated with reductions in unemployment among persons with serious mental disorders. And as productive activities and competitive employment are added to the treatment plans of persons with serious mental disorders, other forms of adjustment improve as well. Once return to productive activities or competitive employment occurs, then social interactions increase, symptoms decrease, and medical and mental health indicators improve (Anthony, Cohen, and Danley, 1988; Bell, Lysaker, and Milstein, 1996; Bell, Milstein, and Lysaker, 1993; Bond, Drake, Becker, and Mueser, 1999; Drake and Mueser, 2000).

There are new contexts and new environments in which reliable and valid principles of vocational rehabilitation are being applied. Moreover, there is a renewed confidence among clinicians, perhaps inspired by the success in pharmacotherapies, to move beyond custodial care and try rehabilitation techniques. And it is not pharmacotherapies alone that make it possible to consider vocational rehabilitation. Changes have occurred in mental health services delivery as a result of managed care practices. Reduced inpatient stays and a shift in the locus of care to community-based programs have created conditions favorable to adding vocational rehabilitation to plans for treating persons with such serious mental disorders as schizophrenia.

Finally, our current national economic expansion, with many new jobs and not enough people to work, has changed attitudes about who is suitable to work. More than anything else, our booming economy has reduced the stigma against employing persons with serious mental disorders.

Although the work therapies being used today have a long history in vocational rehabilitation, the context of their use is quite new: favorable economic conditions, new medications, new technologies, a deemphasis on long-term hospitalization, a new emphasis on community-based services, and renewed confidence that persons in recovery are treated best in the least restrictive environments. The mental health delivery system has changed from inpatient to community-based services, from provider-centered services to an emphasis on mainstream employment (Bond, Drake, Becker, and Mueser, 1999).

And arising from all these many changes is another emerging concept: that of a continuum of rehabilitation. There is a rich variety of services for persons in recovery as they evolve in needs and independence and in choice during rehabilitation. Integral to this continuum is the basic principle of rehabilitation that persons in recovery must have choice, they must be active partners in designing their recovery, and they must choose, get, and keep work (Anthony, Cohen, and Danley, 1988; Danley and Anthony, 1987).

The major points on this continuum of rehabilitation landscape are from the traditional approaches of incentive workshops in highly structured inpatient settings (Luo and Yu, 1994; Sauter and Nevid, 1991); to newer models of transitional work in which patients work alongside staff in hospitals where they are hospitalized or in clubhouses (Beard, Propst, and Malamud, 1982); to the newest models of supported employment and supported education in which staff coach patients who have been placed in mainstream employment in order to give them specialized support so they remain on the job (Bond, 1997; Drake, McHugo, Becker, and Anthony, 1996; Li and Wang, 1994; Cook and Solomon, 1993).

What is new in vocational rehabilitation for the treatment and rehabilitation of persons with serious mental disorders is the notion of stages to which persons in recovery may be matched; that is, persons in recovery choose the work environment that best suits their current needs and their choices. Therefore, when planning treatment, clinicians now think about the contexts of work experiences that the person in recovery may need as that person proceeds through stages of rehabilitation. The continuum goes from work that is suitable for the acute phase of the disorder, when symptoms are less well controlled; to work that is more suitable for a stabilization phase, when symptom management is instituted; and to work that is appropriate for a remission phase, when social connections are reestablished. Sometimes relapses occur, and the cycle of acute phase, to stabilization, to reconnecting with others occurs again. Variations also occur in the kinds of work selected, such as sheltered workshops in inpatient settings to match the acute phase of the disorder, transitional work experiences for the stabilization phase, and therapeutic employment placement in mainstream employment, with job coaching, when persons in recovery are ready to work in the community.

The major variables defining the stages along this continuum of vocational rehabilitation are the concepts of structured/unstructured and dependence/independence. Structured/unstructured refers to the characteristics of the environment and the amount of direction that must be supplied in order for the person to achieve work objectives. Dependence/independence refers to characteristics of the individual and the extent the person relies on others for support in order to complete work tasks. The continuum of rehabilitation and the jobs that comprise this continuum vary from the structured with dependence to the unstructured with independence. Sheltered workshops and incentive therapy programs in hospitals define the structured, dependence end of the continuum, and mainstream employment defines the unstructured, independence end of the continuum.

This concept of a continuum in rehabilitation means that it is highly likely that persons will evolve through stages in their recovery. The end of vocational rehabilitation is not just to get a job but for the person in recovery to continually be choosing, getting, and keeping jobs that are appropriate to his or her current stage in recovery, jobs skills, and work experiences.

The new direction in vocational rehabilitation is this emphasis on a graduated course of recovery along a continuum of rehabilitation differing by structure and by dependence, interacting with personal and vocational adjustment. During the acute phase of the mental disorder, rehabilitation and work need to be more highly structured, such as occurs in inpatient hospitalization when controls are instituted to ensure safety and provide a place of refuge for healing. At such times, persons are most dependent on the treatment setting for support and for management from others for their well-being. But even during acute phases of mental disorders, participation in productive activities may be chosen and may be recommended as an important activity for setting the stage to reentry into the world of work.

As symptoms stabilize and persons feel better able to manage their symptoms and cope with their problems, they require less structured settings of semi-independence in which to function (such as is found in day hospitals, therapeutic residences, or clubhouses). Persons in recovery then become more active agents in choosing, getting, and keeping the kinds of work to suit the stage in their recovery along a continuum of work environments. Finally, as symptoms subside and persons regain control in the everyday management of their lives and once again are able to provide for themselves, they move into the least structured environment, living independently in the community and supported through case management, psychotherapy, and pharmacotherapies delivered in outpatient settings.

Psychologists who work in vocational rehabilitation continually assess the person in recovery with regard to the continuity in rehabilitation. They also bring skills from vocational rehabilitation to the creation of work environments, in particular matching the person in recovery to the most suitable work environment according to stage in recovery. Psychologists subscribe to a rehabilitation tradition that places the person in recovery at the center in making choices about possible productive activities and employment. They can also provide standardized assessments for determining the effects of many different variables on stage in recovery with the type of work environment that is needed and is chosen. Such variables include skills, work experiences, functionality, emotional well-being, environmental supports, work demands, aspirations, medical and mental health needs, and environmental resources.

Types of Work Environment

There are three basic groups to consider for the types of work environments and stages in the person's recovery.

Highly Structured Incentive Therapies and Sheltered Workshops. The most structured and least independent forms of work experiences are incentive activities and sheltered workshops integrated into inpatient hospital settings (Luo and Yu, 1994; Sauter and Nevid, 1991). In this model, persons hospitalized in inpatient settings may be paid for work done on the ward. A variation of this form of work is a sheltered workshop on hospital grounds.

At our hospital in Bedford, Massachusetts, we have developed another variation of the inpatient incentive workshop. In our so-called modified community employment model, we contract with nearby companies to bring piecework to the hospital, so that persons can immediately begin doing real work for pay. We believe that even persons who are hospitalized can perform many useful tasks and that the work that they produce merits pay beginning at the current minimum wage rates. Certain piece-rate jobs take time to master, and so it may take awhile to get up to speed, say, in a job like stethoscope assembly or packaging materials for shipping. But we encourage all hospitalized patients who are able to spend part of their day earning money. We have developed assessment techniques to determine when persons referred for our services should enter such incentive activities and when they are ready to move along the continuum of rehabilitation to better-paying jobs with more independence.

This controlled environment is supervised by vocational rehabilitation specialists who directly supervise persons who have been referred, continually assessing suitability and quality of work that is produced, and continually providing feedback about results to the person. But the person in recovery is the dominant partner in this collaboration. We expect that by exercising choice, the partner will move to more independent work.

The Less Structured, More Independent Domains of Transitional Work. Transitional work requires more independence in functioning, along with direct supervision by skilled vocational rehabilitation specialists. The best practices of such programs are the transitional work therapies of Morris Bell and Paul Lysaker (Bell, Lysaker, and Milstein, 1996; Bell, Milstein, and Lysaker, 1993). The clubhouse, such as the Fountain

House approach (Dincin, 1975), with its work-ordered day and club-house members assigned to prevocational work crews, is also an excellent model.

Transitional work jobs are usually actual jobs but housed in hospital settings or clubhouses. Persons in recovery are assigned to work with hospital staff outside the ward in other locales of the hospital or work together in teams. If the hospital is large, a large variety of jobs can be offered, from work in food service and facilities management to skilled work in typing and electrical repair.

The purpose of transitional work is to prepare the person in recovery for work in the community. This work approximates work in the community, with the exception that the person in recovery may be working for a supervisor who has been trained by the vocational rehabilitation specialist to work with persons with serious mental disorders. Also, support groups are offered for discussing problems encountered on the job and learning ways to improve.

Such transitional work experiences have many advantages. Those on the treatment teams can see how persons in recovery are functioning in real work experiences where demands are made on them and completing tasks is expected. Transitional work can be excellent preparation for applying for work in the community, once the person in recovery has gained the confidence needed to function independently with less structure.

As Bell and others have pointed out (Bell, Lysaker, and Milstein, 1996; Bell, Milstein, and Lysaker, 1993), when work expectation is rewarded or reinforced by pay, the pay itself becomes a strong incentive to continue working. Bell has documented the highly positive impact of earning wages on increasing the participation of persons in recovery in transitional work programs. And as participation increases and more pay is earned, Bell and his colleagues have empirically demonstrated, symptoms decrease and other adjustment indicators improve. We too have documented that once persons with serious mental disorders are enrolled in our form of transitional work, both inpatient days and outpatient visits are reduced (Rosenheck, Frisman, and Sindelar, 1995; Rosenheck and Seibyl, 1998).

The variations of the transitional work therapy model that we are successfully operating at Bedford are based on contracts with local companies and businesses. We negotiate to bring into the medical center work that is comparable to skills required by similar work in the community. Through this work, persons in recovery develop skills that are readily transferable to supported employment. For example, we have established a stethoscope assembly operation as a transitional employment model. Once persons in recovery demonstrate proficiency, the host company hires them for their nearby work site.

The Least Structured and Most Independent World of Supported Therapeutic Employment in the Community. The most recent of the models of supported employment in the community is the individual placement and support (IPS) model (Drake and others, 1996). This model is less structured than transitional work or sheltered workshops and requires more independence on the part of the person in recovery. As a consequence, this model is placed at the other end of the continuum from incentive therapies in inpatient units of state hospitals or Veterans Administration (VA) medical centers.

The IPS model centers its approach in choose-get-keep approaches (Danley and Anthony, 1987) but delivers its vocational rehabilitation through intensive case management services—in this instance, intensive case management that minimizes prevocational testing and training and quickly assigns persons in recovery to work settings, with unlimited support from case managers to remain in the work setting until all difficulties that threaten employment are resolved (Bond, Drake, Becker, and Mueser, 1999).

The variation that we use in Bedford is to create our own businesses, such as a vet construction team. Vocational rehabilitation specialists bid on construction projects for agencies (such as the Department of Defense) and nearby corporations and businesses. From overhead and expenses charged in completing construction projects, we are able to hire project managers who are experienced in teaching persons in recovery new construction skills (or help them to regain lost construction skills) and know how to cope with psychological problems that may interfere with the implementation of such skills. Our medical center pays one vocational rehabilitation specialist to manage the vet construction team, which in fiscal year 2000 will have paid out over $2 million in wages for an average workload of fifty persons in recovery per day, earning an average of twenty dollars an hour in construction wages, supervised by fifteen managers who are paid not by the medical center but by the agencies or companies paying for the construction wages.

Threats to Achieving Independence in Work

There are at least three threats that clinicians must help persons in recovery work through so that they can achieve more independence in functioning and in work.

First, there are deficiencies in requisite skills needed to keep pace in a rapidly expanding economy and in a work environment changing from production based to services and technology based. This means that vocational rehabilitation services must include supported education (Cook and Solomon, 1993). Continuing education must be a fact of life for any person in recovery. And treatment and rehabilitation plans must include supported education and job retraining when needed, when appropriate, and when chosen. Skills needed to keep pace with a rapidly changing job market require continuing mastery of existing skills and constantly adding new skills. Continuing education is especially necessary for those who may have periodic interruptions in work habits and work skills. We offer computer skills training in our medical center even for persons in acute stages of their mental disorders.

Second, substance abuse constitutes one of the major threats to recovery. Surveys show that more than half of persons with serious mental disorders also meet lifetime criteria for substance abuse and that nearly one-third of any sample studied meet current criteria for co-occurring substance abuse (Drake and others, 1998; Drake and Mueser, 2000; Mueser, Drake, and Noordsy, 1998; Mueser, Drake, and Wallach, 1998). Hence, addictions treatment must be integrated into vocational rehabilitation services. Many work environments place persons in recovery at risk, a risk that increases if substances continue to be abused. At each level along the continuum of rehabilitation, persons in recovery who have a history of substance abuse must continue their participation in treatment for addictions.

Third, one of the hidden problems among so many persons in recovery, especially those who meet criteria for schizophrenia, is untreated, co-occurring posttraumatic stress disorder (PTSD; Penk and Flannery, 2000a and 2000b). We hypothesize that failure to offer treatment for PTSD to persons in recovery leads to learned helplessness-like conditions for which custodial approaches to care simply reinforce and reward. We further hypothesize that work experiences provide antidotes for learned helplessness in at least three ways. Work enables traumatized persons to overcome the pervading sense of helplessness in controlling their environment that results from being traumatized. It helps those who have been traumatized develop new reasons for living, reasons that usually have been challenged by memories of trauma that are hard to control and manage. Finally, work usually helps overcome symptoms of avoidance of reminders of trauma and especially symptoms of social withdrawal that frequently accompany not just residuals of trauma but also schizophrenia.

Conclusion

If clinicians are able to integrate traditional treatment services, such as group and individual therapies, pharmacotherapies, and marriage and family therapies into vocational rehabilitation, then the new forms of services delivery that are required by the new millennium will be achieved.

Psychologists need to bring reliable and valid principles of recovery to new settings. We must practice our craft not just in clinics or on hospital wards or in private offices but at the work site too. Many persons in recovery are taught how to adjust to long-term treatment settings in inpatient wards. We must extend principles of learning to cope and to adjust to work sites and work settings. Economic and administrative events are taking psychologists out of the office, the clinic, and the hospital and are providing challenges to reinvent and rediscover the principles of our practice on the job in work environments. It is by centering ourselves and those who entrust us with their care in work that we address the second set of criteria for classifying mental disorders that for so long have been extensively ignored.

So we end where we started, with the mission statement from Sigmund Freud in the twentieth century to those who must pioneer new directions in treatment in the twenty-first century by transferring our technologies from clinics and the office to the world of work: "No other technique for the conduct of life attaches the individual so firmly to reality as laying emphasis on work; for work at least gives one a secure place in a portion of reality in the human community."

References

Anthony, W. A., Cohen, M. R., and Danley, K. S. "The Psychiatric Rehabilitation Approach as Applied to Vocational Rehabilitation." In J. A. Ciardiello and M. D. Bell (eds.), *Vocational Rehabilitation of Persons with Prolonged Psychiatric Disorder*. Baltimore, Md.: Johns Hopkins University Press, 1988.

Anthony, W. A., Rogers, E. S., Cohen, M., and Davies, R. R. "Relationships Between Psychiatric Symptomatology, Work Skills, and Future Vocational Performance." *Psychiatric Services*, 1995, 46(4), 353–358.

Beard, J. H., Propst, R. N., and Malamud, T. J. "The Fountain House Model of Rehabilitation." *Psychosocial Rehabilitation Journal*, 1982, 5, 47–53.

Bell, M., and Lysaker, P. "Levels of Expectation for Work Activity in Schizophrenia: Clinical and Rehabilitation Outcomes." *Psychiatric Rehabilitation*, 1995, 19(3), 71–76.

Bell, M. D., Lysaker, P. H., and Milstein, R. M. "Clinical Benefits of Paid Work Activity in Schizophrenia." *Schizophrenia Bulletin*, 1996, 22(1), 51–67.

Bell, M. D., Milstein, R. M., and Lysaker, P. H. "Pay and Participation in Work Activity: Clinical Benefits for Clients with Schizophrenia." *Psychosocial Rehabilitation*, 1993, 17(2), 173–177.

Bond, G. D. R. "An Update on Supported Employment for People with Severe Mental Illness." *Psychiatric Services*, 1997, 48(3), 335–345.

Bond, G. D. R., Drake, R. E., Becker, D. R., and Mueser, K. T. "Effectiveness of Psychiatric Rehabilitation Approaches for Employment of People with Severe Mental Illness." *Journal of Disability Policy Studies*, 1999, 10(1), 18–52.

Cook, J. A., and Solomon, M. L. "The Community Scholar Program: An Outcome Study of Supported Education for Students with Severe Mental Illness." *Psychosocial Rehabilitation Journal*, 1993, 17, 83–97.

Danley, K. S., and Anthony, W. A. "The Choose-Get-Keep Model: Serving Severely Psychiatric Disabled People." *American Rehabilitation*, 1987, 13, 6–9, 27–29.

Dincin, J. "Psychiatric Rehabilitation." *Schizophrenia Bulletin*, 1975, 1, 131–148.

Drake, R. E., McHugo, G. J., Becker, D. R., and Anthony, W. A. "The New Hampshire Study of Supported Employment for People with Severe Mental Illness." *Consulting and Clinical Psychology*, 1996, 64(2), 391–399.

Drake, R. E., and Mueser, K. T. "Psychosocial Approaches to Dual Diagnosis." *Schizophrenia Bulletin*, 2000, 26, 105–118.

Drake, R. E., and others. "Review of Integrated Mental Health and Substance Abuse Treatment for Patients with Dual Disorders." *Schizophrenia Bulletin*, 1998, 24, 589–608.

Li, F., and Wang, M. "A Behavioral Training Programme for Chronic Schizophrenia Patients: A Three-Month Randomised Controlled Trial in Beijing." *British Journal of Psychiatry*, 1994, 165 (Suppl. 24), 58–67.

Luo, K., and Yu, D. "Enterprise-Based Sheltered Workshops in Nanjing: A New Model for the Community Rehabilitation of Mentally Ill Workers." *British Journal of Psychiatry*, 1994, 165(Suppl. 24), 89–95.

Mueser, K. T., Drake, R. E., and Noordsy, D. L. "Integrated Mental Health and Substance Abuse Treatment for Severe Psychiatric Disorders." *Practical Psychiatry and Behavioral Health,* 1998, *4,* 129–139.

Mueser, K. T., Drake, R. E., and Wallach, M. A. "Dual Diagnosis: A Review of Etiological Theories." *Addictive Behaviors,* 1998, *23,* 717–734.

National Institute on Disability and Rehabilitation Research. *NDDR Consensus Validation Conference: Strategies to Secure and Maintain Employment for Persons with Long-Term Mental Illness, 1992.* Washington D.C.: U.S. Department of Education.

Penk, W. E., and Flannery, R. B. "Literature Review of Treatment Approaches for PTSD: Psychosocial Rehabilitation." In E. B. Foa, T. M. Keane, and M. J. Friedman (eds.), *Effective Treatment for PTSD.* New York: Guilford Press, 2000a.

Penk, W. E., and Flannery, R. B. "Treatment Guidelines for PTSD: Psychosocial Rehabilitation." In E. B. Foa, T. M. Keane, and M. J. Friedman (eds.), *Effective Treatment for PTSD.* New York: Guilford Press, 2000b.

Rosenheck, R., Frisman, L., and Sindelar, J. "Disability Compensation and Work Among Veterans with Psychiatric and Non-Psychiatric Impairments." *Psychiatric Services,* 1995, *46*(4), 359–365.

Rosenheck, R., and Seibyl, C. L. "Participation and Outcome in a Residential Treatment and Work Therapy Program for Addictive Disorders: The Effects of Race." *American Journal of Psychiatry,* 1998, *155,* 1029–1034.

Sauter, A. W., and Nevid, J. S. "Work Skills Training with Chronic Schizophrenic Sheltered Workers." *Rehabilitation Psychology,* 1991, *36*(4), 255–264.

Spaniol, L., Gagne, C., and Koehler, M. (eds.). *Psychological and Social Aspects of Psychiatric Disability.* Boston: Center for Psychiatric Rehabilitation, Boston University, 1997.

Additional References

Drake, R. E. "The New Hampshire Study of Supported Employment for People with Severe Mental Illness." *Journal of Consulting and Clinical Psychology,* 1996, *64,* 390–398.

International Association of Psychosocial Rehabilitation Services (eds.). *An Introduction to Psychiatric Rehabilitation.* Columbia, Md.: IAPSRS, 1994.

Katz, L. J. "Interagency Collaboration in the Rehabilitation of Persons with Psychiatric Disabilities." *Journal of Vocational Rehabilitation,* 1991, *1,* 45–57.

Lysaker, P., Bell, M., Milstein, R., and Bryson, G. "Work Capacity in Schizophrenia." *Hospital and Community Psychiatry,* 1993, *44*(3), 278–280.

Mueser, K. T., Bond, G. R., Drake, R. E., and Resnick, S. G. "Models of Community Care for Severe Mental Illness: A Review of Research on Case Management." *Schizophrenia Bulletin,* 1998, *24,* 37–74.

Mueser, K. T., and Glynn, S. M. *Behavioral Family Therapy for Psychiatric Disorders.* (2nd ed.) Oakland, Calif.: New Harbinger Press, 1999.

Rogers, E. S., Anthony, W. A., Toole, J., and Brown, M. A. "Vocational Outcomes Following Psychosocial Rehabilitation: A Longitudinal Study of Three Programs." *Journal of Vocational Rehabilitation,* 1991, *1*(3), 21–29.

Rutman, I. "How Psychiatric Disability Expresses Itself as a Barrier to Employment." *Psychosocial Rehabilitation Journal,* 1994, *14,* 7–18.

Xie, H., Dain, B. J., Becker, D. R., and Drake, R. E. "Job Tenure Among Persons with Severe Mental Illness." *Rehabilitation Counseling Bulletin,* 1997, *40*(4), 230–239.

WALTER ERICH PENK *is chief of the psychology and compensated work therapy services at the Edith Nourse Rogers Memorial Veterans Hospital in Bedford, Massachusetts.*

3

This chapter describes how the author, who at the time was a practicing psychologist, became personally involved in advocacy for persons with mental illness. He also gives an overview of the activities of several organizations that are, or should be, advocating for this vulnerable population. He describes several specific programs that he sees as exemplary. Finally, the author argues for an approach for improving care, which he feels family and consumer advocates can be particularly effective in implementing.

On Giving Up on the Mental Health System

Dale L. Johnson

I am profoundly pessimistic about the possibility of having effective mental health services in America given what I know about our system. I have thought about the matter for a long time and have tried to find the bright side. I have searched for ways of implementing what we know works best for people with serious mental illness, but I cannot see a way to bring these best practices into the system (Johnson, 1994). We have an ineffective, uncaring, cruel, inhuman system, and no one with the power to make changes seems to care about trying to make it better.

Instead of realizing that having 40 million Americans without health care is a national shame, politicians of both stripes have gone on to minutiae, meanwhile taking great care not to offend the managed care companies, the health insurance companies, or the pharmaceutical industry. Forget the person who has a serious mental illness; the illnesses probably came about because of something the person did to himself or herself (perhaps illegal drugs); or came about because the person was inferior in some way, unable to compete as expected in pursuit of the almighty dollar. Whatever the reason, there is little evidence that anyone in high office at the national, state, or local level cares at all about people with serious mental illness. Ours is the only developed country without a national mental health policy. We leave policy to the states, and they just leave it. In the two states I know best, New Mexico and Texas, a person who seeks help in the public sector can expect to receive a hurried evaluation of his or her problem and a prescription of medication, usually for one of the older and less acceptable types. Both states are thriving and have budget surpluses, but in the area of mental illness, costs are cut and money saved. We spend state money on prisons, highways, and salaries for bureaucrats, but not on services for people with serious mental illnesses.

Our mental health system today is in essentially the same position in which the Soviets found themselves in the mid-1980s, corrupt and nonproductive. Evidence of corruption appears from time to time in the newspapers, and family members suspect there is much more that does not reach the eyes of district attorneys or journalists. My perception of productivity is entirely subjective because no community facility or state program in the nation reports its outcome results, and many do not even collect outcome data. The National Alliance for the Mentally Ill (NAMI), under the leadership of Fuller Torrey, did evaluations of state programs in 1986, 1988, and 1990, but these were discontinued, and this valuable source of information is no longer available. In this era of managed care, the performance of mental health providers is essentially a secret or, more likely, is simply not known.

My Involvement

My dissertation at the University of Kansas was on schizophrenia, and my first job at the Veterans Administration (VA) Hospital in Houston was on a closed unit in which most of the patients had schizophrenia. After a year or two I moved within the hospital to head a research program, then drifted across the bayou to the University of Houston to take a position in developmental psychology. For me, schizophrenia was now to be only a chapter in a textbook in abnormal psychology. I had no intention of spending time with people with serious mental illness, not because I did not like the people or that kind of work—quite to the contrary—but because I had other plans. I had extended my early work on cross-cultural psychology into the field of prevention and planned a series of preventive activities with Mexican American families with young children. These career plans were brought up short in 1972 when my older son, then nineteen years old, developed schizophrenia.

I continued my work on the primary prevention of school failure and behavior problems but gradually moved away from developmental and into clinical work. I changed the courses I was offering: from child development to abnormal psychology, from social development to community treatment of people with serious mental illness, and so forth. The big changes came about for me when we formed a family advocacy group in Houston, and then we discovered and joined NAMI. Our local group did well. We were among the first NAMI groups in the nation to include consumers in meetings and on our board, and we had some successes as advocates. In rapid succession, my wife, Carmen, helped form the Texas Alliance for the Mentally Ill and became president, and I was elected to the NAMI board. I served on it for seven years and was president one year. After that I became more active with the World Schizophrenia Fellowship, now called World Fellowship for Schizophrenia and Allied Disorders, and am now the president elect.

Involvement with these family organizations led to a little research and a lot of writing about families and serious mental illness and about training mental health professionals, chiefly psychologists, to work with this group. It has been a major concern of mine all along to bring NAMI and psychology closer together. As part of that concern I am currently chair of the American Psychological Association Task Force on Serious Mental Illness, which has as one of its missions the promotion of psychology in this field. I have continued to function as an advocate, knowing that better services are possible and for a considerable time was certain that in some way they would become available. It has finally become apparent to me that this optimistic advocacy is unrealistic. There has been too little to give it justification.

Our son rejected his schizophrenia for the first ten years of the disorder, and he was not a compliant patient. His illness was turbulent. By our count he was committed to the state hospital three times, was jailed four times, attempted suicide twice, and was missing (from our point view) or homeless (from his point of view) six times. He was prescribed a broad range of medications and electroconvulsive therapy. He was in group therapy so often he said he had run out of things to say. Everything changed after a particularly damaging psychotic episode and a long period in the state hospital. Finally, with the help of a benevolent group home able to function because California supplements Supplemental Security Income (SSI) and because of the newly approved medication clozapine, he began to improve. This improvement continues today, and he has not been hospitalized for twenty years. He does not work, but he is sociable, works out at the health club, and seems quite content. He has not "recovered"; there is still considerable evidence of negative symptoms.

Did any aspect of the mental health system help him? I do not think he was helped at all by the system as it exists and has existed in Texas or New Mexico. I could list the treatment errors, neglect, and callous indifference that he experienced in Texas. The state hospital was useful at one time, but with the exception of the unit psychiatrist and one or two nurses, the staff had no idea of a treatment plan, evaluation was irrelevant, and attempted rape by a male social worker did not help the recovery process. Housing in Texas and New Mexico is deplorable; neither state supplements SSI payments, and providers cannot survive on the low payments. There were no viable psychosocial treatment programs. Both states have Republican governors who have instituted managed care for the public mental health system, and what were among the poorest systems in the nation (Torrey, Erdman, Wolfe, and Flynn, 1990) have fallen into the abyss. Unfortunately, so have other states.

State of Knowledge

One of the reasons that the service delivery system is so unacceptable is that we now have a range of effective treatment and rehabilitation modes, but they are not being used. These include Fairweather Lodges; Assertive Community Treatment; supported employment; cognitive behavior therapy for schizophrenia, bipolar disorder, and depression; family psychoeducation (for example, Falloon's Optimal Treatment Program); and social learning programs. There are others, but these come to mind because they have strong research support. We also have somewhat improved medications for psychotic, depressive, manic, anxiety, and obsessive symptoms. Directors and staff of community mental health centers, hospitals, and other mental health system agencies seem not to be aware of these modalities (Lehman and others, 1998). In addition, the current system, with its emphasis on short-term cost saving, is unwilling to provide these treatments or services.

It is deplorable that we have no data on how people with serious mental illness are faring. We know that people with acquired immune deficiency syndrome live longer today than they did fifteen years ago, but we do not know if there are changes in longevity for people with schizophrenia. We do not know, in the United States, what the incidence of schizophrenia or bipolar disorder is. These data are collected in some other countries. Here, providers are not required to report data on serious mental illness, although they do report the incidence data for many other illnesses.

The Role of Government and Nongovernment Organizations

National Alliance for the Mentally Ill. NAMI is a large organization that has had some impact on important governmental policies and actions at the national, state, and local levels. One such positive influence was the return of the National Institute of Mental Health (NIMH) to the National Institutes of Health. This has resulted in better research and a more responsive position with regard to serious mental illness. NAMI has also had a strong influence on the adoption of improved insurance parity laws enacted by state governments. Nevertheless, it has had no influence on the growth of managed care, and its leaders were very slow to realize how destructive this movement has been for people with serious mental illness in need of services.

At the state level, many organizations are unable to act with any degree of effectiveness. These state organizations often receive funding from the state division of mental health for operating expenses and special projects, and members are unwilling to risk loss of these funds if they criticize state policies. They remain silent and tell themselves they are doing the right thing.

In my opinion NAMI should develop a national mental health plan. It would be stronger if it was based on a national single-payer system for health care with universal coverage, but this is not essential. It is important that we have a national plan for care for people with serious mental illness.

This plan should ensure basic living supports for all people in need: housing, food, and transportation. These basic elements are ensured in some states, notably those that supplement SSI and Supplemental Security Disability Income (SSDI), but the new plan should require that it be available in every state. The plan should also ensure that complete treatment and rehabilitation services are readily available.

A working national mental health plan may take years to implement. In the meantime, there is more that NAMI should do now. First, it can restore the NAMI Curriculum and Training Committee to carry out two functions:

Establish proficiency credentials for mental health professionals. Professionals could apply to NAMI for credentials to show that they have the training and experience that they need to do their work well. NAMI would establish standards, judge applications, and issue certificates.

Present training through thorough, practical workshops on evidence-based treatments for serious mental illness. For example, no one in the United States now provides training for cognitive-behavioral therapy for the positive symptoms of schizophrenia despite the mass of evidence showing its effectiveness. The same is true of family psychoeducation, as in Falloon's Optimal Treatment Program. NAMI has made an excellent start with its Family to Family program, but that should be regarded as introductory to the Optimal Treatment Program. There are other examples of evidence-based treatments that NAMI should promote.

NAMI might emulate the Association for Retarded Citizens in helping its members develop housing and community services for people with serious mental illnesses. This line of action has been discussed many times, but apparently NAMI members have not been willing to make this leap into action. We have waited long enough for the mental health system to respond. Let us do it ourselves.

Finally, NAMI should develop recovery modules and deliver them in a way similar to the Family to Family program. Volunteer family members and consumers should help other families carry out a program of cognitive stimulation that will help people overcome cognitive deficits and move toward recovery.

American Psychological Association. There is a history of APA leaders and members showing their distaste for anything having to do with serious mental illness by attacking NAMI. It may be significant that the last major development of a psychosocial treatment program for people with serious mental illness by an APA member was more than twenty years ago. This appears to mean that the membership of this large organization is not very interested in mental illness, but it has potential for doing great things.

American Psychological Society. Members are proud of the purity of their science, but they take only rare and brief glimpses at the world of problems outside their laboratories. We would wait long for action from this group. Nevertheless, the potential benefit from basic behavioral science is great.

American Psychiatric Association. Someone has remarked that this organization has a serious drug addiction, complete with withdrawal symptoms and increasing tolerance. We should not despise them for this. It is an attempt to overcome an even worse addiction, psychoanalysis. Psychiatrists, their numbers declining at a high rate, seem content with their prescription-writing role. Medications are important. We can hope that they will become more effective and less noxious, and we will want the psychiatrists to administer them with expert skill.

National Institute of Mental Health. NIMH leaders and staff should read their own committee reports on treatment and services, prevention, and translation of basic research on a monthly basis and check to see if their recommendations are being carried forward. If they are, people with serious mental illness are more likely to be helped in the future.

NIMH's neuroscience program is very important and should be carried on, but it is a long-range program, and it is not likely that anything will come from it that will be of benefit to people in the next decade or even longer. NIMH should expand and accelerate its program of research funding to develop and promote better psychosocial methods. Only 4 percent of its psychosocial research funds are for research in the area of schizophrenia. Bipolar disorder fares no better. This is unacceptable, but it is only partly a problem of NIMH. A major reason for this scant research is that proposals are not forthcoming. Researchers have not been drawn to the area. The time is ripe, and the need urgent, for research in several behavioral research areas.

Center for Mental Health Services. CMHS needs to rethink its research and program development priorities. It has sponsored supported housing, and this form of housing is good for some well-functioning people who have their own complex social systems, but it is not good for people who are withdrawn, suffer from negative symptoms, and have a cognitive deficit. These people need the social stimulation more common in group homes. In addition, CMHS needs to promote integrated serious mental illness and substance abuse programs. To think of treating these two disorders separately and to expect effectiveness in treatment is counter to all recent research.

Local, Non–Mental Health System Services

Magnificat. In 1968 Rose Mary Badami of Houston, Texas, became aware of the many homeless people in the city and set about acquiring houses for people to live in. Today her organization, called Magnificat, owns thirteen houses, a thrift shop, a soup kitchen, an office building, an attractive park, and a psychosocial clubhouse. Magnificat provides a home for 150 formerly homeless people. About half have a serious mental illness, and most of the others have been released recently from prison.

Magnificat has only two paid employees: Badami, the director, and a woman who handles disability applications. The residents do all other work.

They cook, make appointments, fix plumbing leaks, reroof the houses, provide vegetables from the garden, teach computer skills, and do everything else that needs doing. Nearly everyone works in some way.

The houses are well kept and comfortable, and the food is good. Access to clinic appointments is facilitated by Magnificat transportation. Appointments are kept on time. Residents may stay as long as they want if they abide by the rules, but may be trained for external employment if that is their wish.

Badami made a decision at the beginning to avoid entanglement with the mental health system. She does accept referrals from the system, and residents often receive medication from the local system. Otherwise Magnificat goes its own way. Recently she hired a psychologist consultant to help establish the psychosocial clubhouse.

This program exists in the center of a city, most of it one block from a large community college, yet no one seems to know it is there. The houses are in ordinary neighborhoods and blend into the fabric of those neighborhoods.

The cost to the state and nation is what comes to residents as disability payments: SSI or SSDI. The organization also makes use of food stamps, surplus commodities, and other government supports. However, given that residents do all of the work of maintaining the facilities, costs are minimal. More important, residents from the beginning have the experience of doing something important, and this activity is part of their rehabilitation.

The Gathering Place. Because the county mental health system, charged with serving 3 million people in southeast Texas, seemed unable to develop community services for people with serious mental illness, members of NAMI-Houston themselves established a psychosocial clubhouse.

The Gathering Place was developed slowly and now provides a wide variety of services for its members, as is typical of other psychosocial clubhouses. It does have a professional staff. Raising funds for its continued operation is always a problem, but it has been proven possible.

Other Examples. In Manchester, England, it was believed to be important for people with serious mental illness to be occupied doing something worthwhile even if they were unable to hold competitive employment. The Rover program was developed. A group of former patients, along with a nurse and a gardener, would locate urban properties that had been neglected, obtain permission to upgrade them, and then design and build playgrounds and parks using donated materials. The former patients added to the value of their community, and although they were not paid for their work, their sense of self-worth was enhanced.

Home Treatment

Noncompliance with medication is a major problem for most people with psychotic disorders. The program developed at the University of California at Los Angeles is quite effective in providing the information patients need to develop insight into their illness and to become more compliant (Eckman, Liberman, and Phipps, 1990). Mental health professionals have not adopted the methods, in part because a major amount of time is required. They could be carried out by volunteers, with training, of course, who would conduct the manualized sessions.

We are experimenting with ways to overcome the cognitive deficit found so often in serious mental illness. Clearly some form of cognitive stimulation is necessary, and there must be a great deal of practice over a long time. One way this may be done is to use computer games. They are intriguing and inexpensive and challenge a variety of cognitive processes. We have worked the pinball game that comes with some versions of Windows 95, a shareware shoot-down-the-enemy game, and other games. The games must not be complex, must have a score that can be improved with practice, require some skill, and tap into such cognitive functions as planning, anticipation, attention, and short-term memory.

It would not be hard to generate a long list of productive rehabilitation activities that could be operated by volunteers. Training of the volunteers is necessary, but NAMI has demonstrated that this kind of training of non-professional people is possible.

From Stability to Recovery

Most mental health service providers appear to be content with showing that their clients are stable in the community. That is, they would prefer that clients not suffer an inordinate number of relapses. They have adopted the community living model but given little thought to moving on to a recovery model. By this I mean helping people to be able to function in the community as ordinary persons, free of symptoms with or without medication, and able to cope with stress and misfortune with or without psychological assistance.

Since professionals are not willing to adopt methods that may make it possible for people to recover, such as application of Hogarty's Cognitive Enhancement Therapy (Hogarty & Flesher, 1999) or the cognitive retraining that Spaulding and others (1999) devised, families and consumers will have to do it themselves.

Work with families on expressed emotion has taught us that families can help to reduce environmental stress by avoiding expressions of criticism and hostility (Lam, 1991). It has laid the groundwork for telling families how they can help without being too intrusive. All of this is part of the community living model. Now it is time to move ahead to the recovery model. The question becomes one of what to do.

Recent research in health psychology suggests a way in which families can help to foster recovery. This research has placed emphasis on the relationship of patient and professional in dealing with severe and long-term disorders or illnesses. The clinician structures the course of treatment, and the patient carries it out. Marks (1994) has recently described how this works: "Self-care is a major issue if I have a chronic disease, like diabetes, that requires not just one episode of treatment but permanent, ongoing care, without which I will die. I may have to inject insulin every day, varying the dose according to my response, exercise, and stress; test my urine for sugar and ketones; and carefully monitor my diet. At intervals, the clinician advises me what to do, but in the final analysis it is I who have to carry out the treatment" (p. 20). The situation he described is much like that for people recovering from a serious mental illness.

Marks goes on to show that treatments that require active, ongoing participation by the patient have better outcomes if they have certain characteristics, such as close adherence to the prescribed treatment. This adherence to the regime is improved if people keep records of medication taking, noting in diaries occasions of stress, exercise, and the like. Furthermore, he reported that patients with anxiety disorders do better if they repeatedly confront the feared situations or objects.

How is this relevant for a recovery model? Let us take the idea that Harding's patients did well because they learned how to cope with problems better with the passage of time (Harding and others, 1987). Presumably this coping makes recovery possible. Setting aside our doubts about this for the moment and accepting it as a viable hypothesis about the nature of recovery, we find that it places us right on the health psychology research path. How can professionals, consumers, and family members help the person to cope better? The health psychology research suggests we could help to maintain a prescribed program. But is this not already being done? It is relatives and group home staff who remind the consumer to take medications and go to the psychosocial club. That is true, but the health psychology procedure goes beyond these reminders. It introduces a reason for doing various things and is focused on the consumer's learning to cope better. It is empowerment. Others can help by being prompters, guides, and facilitators.

Consider an example. Alice does well in the community. She takes her medication with only a little reminding, goes to her appointments with some reminding, can manage the blood test routine for clozapine monitoring, likes to eat out and go to movies, and is fairly sociable. But she rarely initiates anything, sleeps quite a bit, sits alone smoking cigarettes, and does not much like the psychosocial club. She continues to be quite sensitive to stress and avoids highly stimulating situations by leaving them.

Let us assume that after an assessment period with Alice and her family carried out by the recovery group comprising NAMI members, there is agreement that Alice could make progress by developing active coping methods rather than resorting exclusively to avoidance. The recovery group develops a plan, and Alice practices elements of it with the clinician. A member of the family agrees to be the helper. For a period of time, Alice will work on developing problem-focused coping, including taking direct action to solve a problem or seeking information that will be important for arriving at a solution. In addition, Alice and the clinician would explore emotion-focused coping: reducing reactions to stress by removing herself from the problem, relaxing, exercising, or seeking comfort from others. Learning effective coping skills requires that the learning process be orderly and that records be kept of the territory explored and the results of trials or personal experiments (Falloon and others, 1998).

Most professional prescriptions are too vague—for example, "Take these pills," "Go to the psychosocial club," or "Learn to cope." In contrast, the methods developed by the health psychologists are highly specific. It is possible for clients to see whether they have achieved something or have experienced failure and to know what to do next to improve their chances of success.

Many people can work with the clinician by themselves. Two problems arise in the case of serious mental illness: one is the difficulty in initiating activities, and the other has to do with judgment or insight. These problems make it unlikely that the client could follow the program prescribed by the health psychologists thoroughly enough to make it effective. That is where the family or other people who are reliably present in the person's life come in. They remind, listen to the data collected by the consumer and to ideas about variations, and provide support. In short, they provide temporary assistance to overcome specific difficulties. In a sense, they are like the seeing eye dog for the person who is blind, the loud telephone for the hearing impaired, and the elevator for the person in a wheelchair. The help makes access to goals possible.

This process can move forward from developing more effective coping methods to dealing with other problems. Work with anxiety disorders, for example, makes it clear that it is essential that people expose themselves to anxiety-provoking situations and make it through the anxiety. This is done not only a few times or in one series of therapy sessions, but provision is made for follow-up restrengthening encounters. A person with a speaker anxiety can be effectively treated with systematic desensitization, but to prevent relapse, he or she must regularly put himself or herself in speaking situations.

Marks (1994) concluded, "Self-care is an increasingly central theme in health care in general and behavior therapy in particular. Most of the behavior therapist's role is to help patients devise an appropriate strategy to overcome the problem, execute the strategy systematically, and subsequently prevent relapse" (p. 20). He then discusses noncooperative clients and admits that they continue to be a problem. It is here that the family or others close to the ill family member play a vital role.

Families in general support the idea of recovery. They hold it in their minds as a possibility even when it seems impossible. They have seen the person with mental illness before the illness began, and they know what that person has done and think that this could be accomplished again.

Many have come to accept any improvement as a reason for giving thanks, but recovery continues to be the desired goal.

I wrote the several paragraphs above for a conference in Ohio on recovery several years ago. Subsequently I have taken Falloon's Optimal Treatment Program workshop (Falloon and others, 1998) and discovered that there are close similarities. I suggest now that NAMI apply the methods developed for Family to Family and extend them to the Optimal Treatment Program. It could be done, and done free of fumbling by community mental health center staff. Most important, it would be done.

Conclusion

It is time to say, "Up against the wall, systems despots. We have had enough of your endless incompetence, your corrupt practices, your ignorance, and your gross negligence of people with serious mental illness. We want you out of business, at least until the nation adopts a workable, enforceable program of care; then perhaps, if you have upgraded your competence, you might be able to return." In the meantime, we consumers and families and our friends will have to do it ourselves. We must work together, because no one can deal with serious mental illness entirely alone. The need is urgent, and we have the capabilities. In the words of my grandfather's Non-Partisan League, "We won't quit; we will win."

References

American Psychiatric Association. *Diagnostic and Statistical Manual of Mental Disorders.* (3rd ed., rev.) Washington, D.C.: American Psychiatric Press, 1987.

Barrowclough, C., and Tarrier, N. "Recovery from Mental Illness: Following It Through with a Family." In C. Patmore (ed.), *Living After Mental Illness: Innovations in Services.* London: Croom Helm, 1987.

Barton, R. "The Rehabilitation-Recovery Paradigm: A Statement of Philosophy for a Public Mental Health System." *Psychiatric Rehabilitation Skills,* 1998, *2,* 171–187.

Eckman, T. A., Liberman, R. P., and Phipps, C. C. "Teaching Medication Management Skills to Schizophrenic Patients." *Journal of Clinical Psychopharmacology,* 1990, *10,* 33–38.

Falloon, I.R.H. "Early Intervention for First Episodes of Schizophrenia: A Preliminary Exploration." *Psychiatry,* 1992, *55,* 4–15.

Falloon, I.R.H., and others. "Optimal Treatment Strategies to Enhance Recovery from Schizophrenia." *Australian and New Zealand Journal of Psychiatry,* 1998, *32,* 43–49.

Harding, C., and others. "The Vermont Longitudinal Study of Persons with Severe Mental Illness: II. Long-Term Outcome of Subjects Who Retrospectively Met DSM-III Criteria for Schizophrenia." *American Journal of Psychiatry,* 1987, *144,* 727–735.

Heinrichs, R. W. "Schizophrenia and the Brain: Conditions for a Neuropsychology of Madness." *American Psychologist,* 1993, *48,* 221–223.

Hogarty, G. E., and Flesher, S. "Practice Principles of Cognitive Enhancement Therapy." *Schizophrenia Bulletin,* 1999, *25,* 693–708.

Johnson, D. L. "Quality Services for the Mentally Ill: Why Psychology and the National Alliance for the Mentally Ill Need Each Other." In D. T. Marsh (ed.), *New Directions in the Psychological Treatment of Serious Mental Illness.* New York: Praeger, 1994.

Lam, D. H. "Psychosocial Family Intervention in Schizophrenia: A Review of Empirical Studies." *Psychological Medicine*, 1991, *21*, 423–441.

Lehman, A. F., and others. "Patterns of Usual Care for Schizophrenia: Initial Results from the Schizophrenia Patient Outcomes Research Team (PORT) Client Survey." *Schizophrenia Bulletin*, 1998, *24*, 11–20.

Marks, I. "Behavior Therapy as an Aid to Self-Care." *Current Directions in Psychological Science*, 1994, *3*, 19–22.

Paul, G. L. *Assessment in Residential Treatment Settings*. Champaign, Ill.: Research Press, 1986.

Spaulding, W. D., and others. "Effects of Cognitive Treatment in Psychiatric Rehabilitation." *Schizophrenia Bulletin*, 1999, *25*, 657–676.

Stein, L. I., & Test, M. A. (eds.). *Training in Community Living Model—A Decade of Experience*. New Directions for Mental Health Services, no. 26. San Francisco: Jossey-Bass, 1985.

Torrey, E. F., Erdman, K., Wolfe, S. M., and Flynn, L. M. *Care of the Seriously Mentally Ill: A Rating of State Programs*. Arlington, Va.: National Alliance for the Mentally Ill, 1990.

Warner, R. *Recovery from Schizophrenia: Psychiatry and Political Economy*. London: Routledge, 1985.

Wyatt, R. J. "Neuroleptics and the Natural Course of Schizophrenia." *Schizophrenia Bulletin*, 1991, *17*, 325–352.

DALE L. JOHNSON *is professor of psychology at the University of Houston. He is a past president of the National Alliance for the Mentally Ill and current president-elect of the World Fellowship for Schizophrenia and Allied Disorders. He is a recent recipient of the American Psychological Association's Harold M. Hildreth Award, which is presented annually "for exceptional achievement and dedication in public service psychology."*

4

The roles of psychology and psychiatry are rapidly changing with respect to people with serious mental illness. The development of these roles will seriously impact the quality of care available for this vulnerable population.

Psychologists, Psychiatrists, and Psychosis: Will Turf Battles Trump Treatment?

Harriet P. Lefley

This chapter explores the current initiative for psychologists' prescribing privileges and the possible effects of this activity on the conceptualization and treatment of psychotic disorders and modes of service delivery. Psychotic episodes are sporadic features of severe and persistent mental illness, a condition requiring not only ongoing medication management but rehabilitative programs and wraparound services as well. Therefore, we are talking about two interrelated types of disorder: a brain pathology treated by medical interventions and a diminished coping capacity and life situation that can only be remedied by behavioral and environmental interventions, including education and modeling by peers.

Because psychotropic medications have always been the province of physicians, the battle with psychiatrists is now joined. Over the years, psychologists have favored working with people other than those with a major psychotic disorder. With all patient populations, however, the discipline itself tends to deemphasize somatic interventions and to focus on psychosocial factors and the remediation of pathological cognitions and learned behaviors. Psychiatrists have always worked with patients with major psychoses, but with varying theoretical approaches. Despite years of focusing on putative psychodynamic etiologies, psychiatrists have always tended to be more biologically oriented and are certainly so today. The medical discipline is more likely to address the neurochemical basis of psychoses, the psychological discipline to deal with the existential problems of coping with severe and persistent mental illness.

NEW DIRECTIONS FOR MENTAL HEALTH SERVICES, no. 88, Winter 2000   © Jossey-Bass

Comparing Psychiatry and Psychology

Psychiatry is a branch of medicine, and all psychiatrists therefore are physicians. They have completed the necessary years of training in all basic aspects of anatomy and physiology, and have had some exposure to a large variety of medical pathologies and to their symptomatic and organic distinctions. They can use and interpret an array of diagnostic tools ranging from bodily products to imaging. They have a strong knowledge of chemistry and are presumed to understand the structure and components of medications and their actions on the human body. Medical students' knowledge of the social and behavioral sciences is largely limited to some didactic courses in human development, basic psychological processes, and social aspects of medicine. Psychiatric training attempts to add psychological and sociocultural materials to this basic introduction, as well as training in various types of psychotherapy and research techniques. The extent and orientation depend on the medical school. Psychiatric or psychosocial rehabilitation is featured in some medical schools but does not appear to be a standardized feature of most curricula.

Psychology is a behavioral science, a bounded discipline in and of itself but with numerous specialties. Social, personality, industrial, experimental, and similar specialties have no essential concern with abnormal behavior or clinical issues. Medical psychologists or behavioral medicine specialists are concerned with patients' psychological experience of a somatic disease and the possible effects of their reactions on its course and prognosis. But they are not usually involved in drug prescriptions for that disease.

Clinical psychology, a discipline with its own track in most training programs, is the specialty solely concerned with psychosis. In practice, graduates of counseling psychology programs frequently act in clinical capacities in public sector facilities that treat persons with psychosis. But by definition their training is not oriented toward this population. Neuropsychologists are the main specialists who may know as much about the human brain as psychiatrists do, but they have tended to focus on diagnostic testing and organic conditions such as the dementias rather than psychosis. Psychologists of all persuasions, however, have been concerned with behavioral and cognitive processes, and they may have contributed to the diagnostic and therapeutic tools used in the treatment and rehabilitation of people with psychotic disorders.

Although most clinical psychology programs require an internship in clinical facilities, these settings do not always serve people with psychotic disorders. Exposure of clinical psychology interns to this population is generally a matter of local emphasis. Also, licensing of psychologists as practitioners varies from state to state. State examinations typically address a range of clinical issues, but eligibility for licensing is not always restricted to graduates of clinical training programs. Psychologists who hold the doctorate in nonclinical specialties and have worked in the mental health field may be grandfathered in. It is entirely possible for a psychologist to have a license and have no background in brain physiology or function.

The divisions of the American Psychological Association may contain nonclinically trained people who deal on a regular basis with persons with psychosis. For example, Psychologists in Public Service has been concerned with the treatment and futures of multiply hospitalized patients in the public sector—those most likely to suffer from psychotic disorders. Forensic and social psychologists may be greatly concerned with the populations of persons with psychosis who are in jail or living on the streets. Most of these psychologists have administrative, diagnostic, or consultant roles. Unless they are directly involved in treatment, professionals trained in these specialties are not likely to want to devote several years of their lives to obtain additional training in order to prescribe medications.

Relative Strengths of the Two Disciplines

Regardless of specialization, the basic education of all psychologists typically involves rigorous training in human development and personality theory to an extent unmatched in medical training. All psychologists who receive the doctorate have been rigorously trained in research. Clinical psychologists have learned to apply and interpret a battery of diagnostic tests, which psychiatrists often use for diagnostic clarity. Clinical psychologists' training in various schools of psychotherapy is typically more comprehensive and rigorous than that of psychiatrists, whose time must be spent on the wards more than in classrooms.

When compared with the training of clinical psychologists, psychiatrists' education is generally more comprehensive in critical areas related to persons with psychosis. First, psychiatric residents have spent most of their time on hospital wards, dealing with patients from the very beginning. Psychiatric training always includes work in crisis emergency units as well as inpatient and outpatient settings with patients with acute and chronic psychotic disorders. Second, they have far greater grounding in the chemistry and applications of psychoactive medications. Third, they have far better grounding in distinguishing mental illnesses from medical conditions that may have psychotic features.

There cannot be any dispute that psychiatrists know more than most psychologists do about the neuropathology of psychosis. They know more about the action of psychotropic medications on the neurotransmitters. They are far more capable of diagnosing comorbidity. Co-occurring medical conditions are a very real problem among people with long-term schizophrenia or bipolar disorder.

The strengths of psychologists lie in the vast psychosocial area of dysfunction that precedes and accompanies the experience of psychosis. Psychologists are better trained in treating the sequelae of psychotic episodes and dealing with the erosion of hopes and loss of skills that are incurred by those with serious and persistent mental illness. Cognitive and behavioral therapies were developed primarily by psychologists, as well as a large array of psychiatric rehabilitation techniques. Regardless of whether diagnostic or treatment approaches are psychodynamic or neurological, they may be informed by appropriate psychological testing.

The Turf Battles

Turf battles are not new to medicine. Physicians are not the only professionals with the legal authority to prescribe drugs. Over the years they have had to contend with encroachments from other medical or quasi-medical disciplines. Advanced nurse practitioners, as well as dentists, podiatrists, optometrists, and other allied specialists, now have limited prescribing privileges. Psychiatrists must also contend with other physicians, the general practitioners who see and dispense drugs to the majority of patients with clinical depression and other forms of mental disorder.

Although encroachment from allied disciplines has typically been fought, these turf battles involved specialists with physiological training and certified expertise in some area of the body. Psychologists, on the other hand, have long maintained that their discipline is essentially behavioral rather than somatic. Thus, many in the medical community interpret the prescription initiative as primarily driven by economics, that is, as a new source of income rather than an addition (and an inadequate and dangerous one at that) to an existing armamentarium of skills.

The battle over prescription rights is heating up. State psychological and psychiatric associations have been investing inordinate amounts of money, time, and attention to either promoting or contesting legislative efforts to grant psychologists prescription rights. In various states, the professional organization of each discipline has hired lobbyists, supported candidates, and otherwise tried to influence state legislators to introduce, support, or combat targeted bills. Although as of this writing no state yet has psychologist prescription privileges, training programs offer several years of continuing education and certification, so that qualified individuals will be ready and available to dispense psychoactive drugs when the requisite legislation has passed. The Prescribing Psychologists' Register, which in April 2000 claimed eleven thousand members, is the oldest national group devoted to this effort. Two newer affiliate organizations are the American College of Advanced Practice Psychologists and the Psychologist Physician's Register.

Publications of each profession regularly report on the progress of this initiative, pro and con. Most state psychological associations have committees either investigating or advocating for prescription privileges. Most state psychiatric associations are prepared to fight any such bills in their legislatures. A lobbyist addressing the American Psychiatric Association's Joint Institute on State Legislative and Public Affairs in February 2000 urged psychiatrists to prepare to fight psychologist-prescribing bills by investing "time, effort, and money in building relationships with state lawmakers, and 'to ferret out other relationships that could be useful'" (Hausman, 2000, p. 43). Psychiatrists were also urged to use direct mail campaigns to the public. A questionnaire would ask a large number of recipients whom they want to be in charge of prescribing complex medications, presumably countering psychologists' lobbying efforts with voters' opposition.

For busy professionals, this degree of investment in turf battles diverts time and attention from more substantive issues, such as patient care and adequate mental health systems. Rarely has there been a sufficiently united front among professionals, service providers, consumers, and citizen advocates when lobbying for mental health resources. This added fragmentation among professionals, with its apparent show of vested interest, further erodes respect and attention from the legislators on whom we rely for basic services.

Changes in Professional Boundaries and Roles

The growth of community mental health centers and removal of mental health care from hospital sites created the first important change in traditional role relationships. Clinical directors who were social workers frequently had authority over psychiatrist medical directors. Executive directors could be of any discipline or even administrators with no mental health training at all. In both private and public sectors, turf issues have emerged among mental health professionals because of overlapping functions and the blurring of disciplinary boundaries. Almost anyone with a degree, including one in counseling from a school of education, can offer psychotherapy to patients with a wide range of diagnoses.

Today with managed care we see changing standards regarding years of training, professional status, and payment for services. There are wholesale revisions of the critical essentials of patient services, their number and duration, and who gets paid for doing what. Inevitably there is a scramble among those who wish to administer the higher-paid services, especially those services that inherently offer more durability and greater job security.

A major argument favoring prescription privileges for psychologists is the avoidance of split roles for therapists. Managed care has created a situation in which psychiatrists prescribe medications and psychologists and social workers dispense psychotherapy. In treating individuals with psychosis, ongoing medication monitoring is essential. Psychotherapy is limited to a certain number of sessions, and its value for persons with psychotic disorders is often contested. Increasingly psychiatrists may be losing their skills as psychotherapists. The annual conferences of the American Psychiatric Association pay considerable attention to the countertherapeutic aspects of split roles, which affect not only patients but psychiatrists as well.

Economics and Paradoxical Paradigm Shifts

The psychological literature has a lot of complaints about the "medicalizing" of mental illness. Despite a mountain of empirical evidence, questions remain about the biological basis of major syndromes such as schizophrenia, bipolar disorder, and other conditions with psychotic features. Objections of "biological reductionism" largely derive from social scientists or others who still subscribe to environmental determinism and the psychosocial etiology of mental disorders. Psychologists have been prominent among these protesters. It is quite paradoxical that so many psychologists now want to participate in the medicalizing of behavioral disorders—to address problem behaviors not through environmental interventions but through dispensing clozapine or selective serotonin reuptake inhibitors or even Ritalin.

Reimbursement schedules for managed care companies and Medicaid functionally limit psychiatrists to medication management and proscribe their dual roles as psychotherapists. Every clinical facility must offer medication management. But psychotherapy is an arbitrary and restricted service. Patients complain that they want somebody to talk to, but the physician may be able to see them for only an allotted ten minutes. This is barely enough time to elicit medication problems or side effects, and never enough time to elicit existential or other psychological concerns.

Patients want to talk about life, work, love, and other adjustment problems and how they can cope with societal stigma and diminished life aspirations. Sometimes they are lucky enough to get a social worker or a master's-level counselor for psychotherapy. But we have no empirical data on the benefits of these dual arrangements and whether in fact it may be countertherapeutic for patients to have to split their allegiances and transferences with different healers. We know only that psychiatrists may be losing their psychotherapeutic skills and that current practice reinforces their identity as medical doctors and undermines their identity as psychological healers.

In all disciplines, moreover, the focus on medication and psychotherapy as the two treatment essentials can be counterproductive. Persons with long-term psychotic conditions have problems that require behavioral remediation in rehabilitative settings. They need information that will enable them to acknowledge and manage their illnesses. Many have lost a substantial number of life skills. They have trouble concentrating, taking transportation, applying for jobs, working, and relating to others in appropriate ways. They need rehabilitation programs, social outlets, psychoeducation about their conditions, job training, supported employment and housing, and mentoring from peers in recovery.

It is ironic that even in universities with centers for research and training in psychiatric rehabilitation, this subdiscipline is rarely a standard component of training in clinical psychology. Psychologists have developed the major components of rehabilitation. Psychological theory and research have been used to develop cognitive and behavioral approaches so that persons with psychotic disorders can retrieve eroded skills or acquire new ones. Social learning theory and its tools have been used for interpersonal skills training so that people can learn to approach others, have a love life, or get jobs. Rehabilitation takes people a jump beyond psychotherapy; it transcends process to create a product needed to enhance one's quality of life, and in so doing, it generates and enhances motivation and insight.

Why then do psychologists focus on learning how to prescribe medications for persons with psychotic disorders rather than helping them enhance their quality of life? Why is there a movement toward a medicalization of psychology? Why do psychiatrists passively accept their assigned role as physicians, abdicating their roles as psychotherapists? Why do the training curricula in both fields eschew any emphasis on rehabilitation? Why is so little attention paid to what is happening in the consumer movements—the research on peer counseling, consumer service providers, and consumer-operated enterprises (Mowbray, Moxley, Jasper, and Howell, 1997)? Why is so little known about the effects of peer mentoring and role modeling, the extraclinical resources for positive identity and self-esteem, and the current focus on the conceptualization, definitions, and process of recovery?

Conclusion

Information abounds on the biological basis of major mental illnesses and the freedoms afforded by appropriate medications. But the right medications are only the beginning of a potentially decent life. Of all the disciplines, psychology has provided the instruments for acquiring rehabilitative skills. Currently the American Psychological Association's new Task Force on Serious Mental Illness is a long-overdue attempt to redirect clinical psychologists toward their original target group, one they have long abandoned. But this task force has had a focus on consumer dialogue, rehabilitation, and recovery. There has been no attention to psychologists' developing prescription skills, and my hope is that this will remain so.

Yet people with serious mental illness need ongoing medication, particularly the newer atypical neuroleptics. Professionals who can prescribe medication are subject to a barrage of influences. Pharmaceutical companies are powerful allies of psychiatrists; they sponsor industry-supported symposia at all major conventions and regional and local meetings. They pay handsomely for noted researchers to give important, state-of-the-art presentations, typically accompanied by free breakfasts, luncheons, or dinners. They pay for grand rounds lecturers in departments of psychiatry. Detail men and women abound in medical schools, providing free samples to residents as well as free lunches, during which they expound on the virtues of their products.

If psychologists acquire prescription privileges, they will benefit equally from this largesse, provided they have a comparable caseload of long-term patients with continuing medication needs. Psychologists' assumption is that the advanced training will be sufficiently rigorous to preclude the dire predictions of medical professionals that increased income may be offset by increased litigation from damaged patients. Physicians fear that many harmful errors may be made in patient care. Without long years of medical training, there is too much danger of misdiagnosing medical diseases with psychotic features, prescribing wrong medications, prescribing wrong dosages, ignoring or misinterpreting potentially toxic interactions, missing symptoms of comorbidity, and similar practice deficiencies.

For psychologists, the offset is an enhanced and profitable role in the treatment of serious mental illness. Together with their extensive academic training in psychotherapy and their research skills, psychologists with prescription privileges arguably may make psychiatry an orphan discipline. Benefits for patients, however, are problematic. Since medication prescription and management is an essential, well-reimbursed treatment modality, psychologists may or may not elect to continue with psychotherapy for an essentially Medicaid population. But without clear reimbursement schedules, they will find it financially unrewarding to learn or pursue cognitive retraining, social skills development, or other time-demanding aspects of psychiatric rehabilitation.

Mental health care has now joined the ranks of managed medical care; it is dollar driven and geared to the lowest level of illness management, the bottom line in profit and in services. Most psychologists and psychiatrists who went into their disciplines hoping to help people with mental illness have long since been forced to abandon their youthful idealism. Of course, maybe if psychiatrists' or psychologists' functions were restricted to crisis management and medication, to essential somatics, the attrition of professionally run systems might enhance the influence of nonprofessional care, expanding the potential of consumers to treat each other. Then maybe consumers would be reimbursed at a rate commensurate with their services, and more would be encouraged to enter the field. But a much more likely scenario would be a diminution of clinical training in serious mental illness and a new abandonment of those who are most needful by the mental health professions: people with psychotic disorders.

The present era offers the traditional components of crisis in the Chinese pictograph: danger and opportunity. The danger is for two critically needed professions to waste their energies and deprive patients of their unique competencies. The opportunity is for the field to develop a comprehensive array of team services in which mental health professionals, rehabilitation specialists, and consumers work together in an integrated system, in which the specialized and generalized skills of psychiatrists and psychologists complement and enrich each other in the service of patient care.

References

Hausman, K. "Lobbyists Recount War Stories from Psychologist-Prescribing Fight." *Psychiatric News,* Apr. 7, 2000, pp. 14, 43.

Mowbray, C. T., Moxley, D. P., Jasper, C. A., and Howell, L. L. *Consumers as Providers in Psychiatric Rehabilitation.* Columbia, Md.: International Association of Psychosocial Rehabilitation Services, 1997.

HARRIET P. LEFLEY is a professor in the Psychiatry Department at the University of Miami School of Medicine. She has long been an active member of the National Alliance for the Mentally Ill and is a recipient of the American Psychological Association's Harold M. Hildreth Award, which is presented annually "for exceptional achievement and dedication in public service psychology."

5

The current emphasis on relapse prevention in serious mental illness offers psychologists new opportunities and roles for which they are uniquely suited.

Relapse Prevention in Serious Mental Illness

David P. Walling, Diane T. Marsh

Beverly is a sixty-two-year-old woman who was diagnosed with schizophrenia nearly thirty-five years ago. She has had multiple hospitalizations over the years and on numerous occasions has spent six months or longer in a locked inpatient facility. She is married, although she and her husband have been separated for a number of years. She has three grown daughters; her youngest daughter (age thirty-four) serves as her primary support. For the past three years, Beverly has been treated in the community without the need for hospitalization or crisis services. During this time, she has worked with a multidisciplinary treatment team that has helped her learn to cope with her symptoms, recognize her symptom triggers, and develop a relapse-prevention plan that she uses to manage her mental illness. Beverly reports that she is now in control of her illness.

In important respects, Beverly does not differ from many other individuals with a serious mental illness who have been treated over the years in institutional settings. Until recently, it was assumed that relapse and hospitalization were part of the normal course of a serious mental illness and that little could be done to prevent their reoccurrence. In fact, prior to the last twenty years, the literature included numerous cases in which relapse and hospitalization were planned events (Green and Rabiner, 1978).

Recent research findings have challenged the myth that relapse is inevitable. Numerous studies have shown that individuals can learn to control many of the symptoms associated with a serious mental illness and that relapse rates can be significantly reduced (Falloon, Roncone, Malm, and Coverdale, 1998). What is different about Beverly's treatment plan is the focus on developing a plan to prevent relapse and the attempt to maintain her in the community. Her success is in large part due to the availability of more effective psychopharmacological and psychosocial interventions, along with a more assertive and hopeful treatment philosophy. As Beverly's case illustrates, individuals with serious mental illness can and do recover.

Understanding Relapse

Serious mental illness is usually marked by periods of remission, when symptoms are absent or well controlled, and of exacerbation, when symptoms return or worsen. Relapse is generally defined as an exacerbation or intensification of symptoms severe enough to interfere with daily living activities (Moller and Murphy, 1997). Relapse prevention is a relatively new concept in the mental health field, particularly so in the area of serious mental illness, which encompasses schizophrenia, bipolar disorder, major depression, and other severe and persistent mental disorders.

Several developments have influenced current thinking about relapse prevention. First, recovery from serious mental illness, once thought impossible, has been repeatedly documented in long-term studies that suggest a life process open to multiple influences and characterized by many outcomes, a majority of them positive (Wasylenki, 1992). In reality, lifetime recovery can be anticipated for at least two-thirds of those who are diagnosed with serious mental illness (Harding, Zubin, and Strauss, 1992; Torrey, 1995). Recovery is also manifested in the productive lives of an increasing number of recovered and recovering people who are open about their experience (see the chapters in this issue by Bassman, Frese, and Siebert). As individuals recover from serious mental illness, the illness becomes simply one life experience that neither defines them as human beings nor places artificial limits on their lives.

Second, researchers have demonstrated that most relapses can be predicted and prevented. In fact, estimates are that as many as 80 percent of relapses may be preventable (Amenson, 1998a). An effective relapse-prevention plan is likely to reduce the risk of costly hospitalizations, as well as the traumatic disruption of individual lives. Although assisting consumers and families to develop such a plan requires more professional time than pharmacotherapy alone, over the course of a year, substantial professional time is saved through reductions in crisis management and hospital care (Falloon and others, 1998).

Third, relapse prevention is enhanced by the availability of new and more effective interventions strategies, including novel pharmacotherapy, Assertive Community Treatment (ACT) programs, and psychosocial models of intervention. Based on results of numerous studies, it is now clear that effective community-based treatment of serious mental illness requires a multimodal approach. Often combining pharmacological and psychosocial therapies produces a synergistic effect that maximizes the prospects for recovery and minimizes the risk of relapse.

The vulnerability-stress model offers a useful framework for understanding and integrating current thinking about serious mental illness. The model also has important implications for relapse prevention.

The Vulnerability-Stress Model

The vulnerability-stress model assumes that serious mental illness involves a vulnerability—or biological predisposition—to develop certain symptoms and that a range of biological and psychosocial factors can interact with this vulnerability to affect the course of the illness. These factors include symptom triggers, which are events that tend to evoke or intensify symptoms; risk factors, which are associated with symptom exacerbation and increased likelihood of relapse; and protective factors, which can reduce (and offer protection from) symptoms of the illness and make relapse less likely. Each component of the model merits consideration in the relapse prevention process.

Vulnerability. Substantial evidence has been amassed that serious mental illnesses are brain disorders marked by alterations in brain activity, chemistry, and structure. As Amenson (1998b) points out, much of our current understanding of biological factors in serious mental illness has resulted from major technological developments that have been available only since the mid-1980s, including brain imaging techniques such as positron emission tomography and nuclear magnetic resonance imaging. A common finding in schizophrenia research is ventricular enlargement, which may indicate that the brain has atrophied or shrunk due to damage or death of some brain cells. Other brain abnormalities have been found in the frontal and temporal lobes, the basal ganglia, and the limbic system.

These neurobiological deficits are associated with certain symptoms and limitations, which may include positive (psychotic) symptoms; negative symptoms, which are characterized by a decline in normal thoughts, experiences, and feelings (for example, lack of motivation or of pleasure); disturbances of mood; severe anxiety; and other disabling symptoms. In addition to symptoms, particular limitations are associated with serious mental illness, including unusual vulnerability to environmental and interpersonal stress, as well as deficiencies in cognitive and social functioning.

Symptom Triggers. Certain events seem to trigger symptoms, almost as if a button is pushed and the symptoms are turned on. Such events, sometimes called symptom triggers, can be unique to the individual, such as an anniversary reaction to a prior trauma, or more commonly associated with symptom return or exacerbation. Symptom triggers can be behaviors, feelings, cognitions, or situations that precede the reappearance or worsening of symptoms. They may be related to medication (for example, skipping doses, stopping medication, changing medication, or taking other medication), use of alcohol and street drugs, or excessive stress (for example, overstimulation or excessive change). Other triggers may involve medical problems, the illness cycle itself, interpersonal conflict, or lifestyle issues. Whatever the specific trigger, the critical factor in the relapse process is the individual's subjective experience.

Risk Factors. A range of biological and psychosocial factors can interact with biologically based vulnerability to affect the course of serious mental illness. Less specific and time limited than symptom triggers, risk factors also increase the likelihood that symptoms will worsen and that a relapse will occur. Such factors include high levels of stress, an unhealthy lifestyle, and substance abuse. Estimates are that over the course of their lives, half of individuals with serious mental illness will have a co-occurring substance abuse problem; the incidence of such comorbidity is approximately 25 percent at any given time (Regier and others, 1990).

Some authors have suggested that consumers with schizophrenia who use substances may prefer those that affect dopamine pathways in the brain (Steinberg, 1994). These substances may alleviate some of the negative symptoms that often accompany both the disorder and the use of conventional antipsychotics. However, the use of alcohol and street drugs may also potentiate the more disruptive positive symptoms and increase cognitive disorganization, poor judgment, perceptual disturbances, and depression. Moreover, as Mueser, Drake, and Wallach (1998) report, because individuals with a serious mental illness are more sensitive to the effects of these substances, they are at greater risk for negative consequences than the general population is.

Protective Factors. Protective factors can reduce symptoms of the illness and make relapse less likely. Examples of such factors are coping skills, family and social support, and medication. Based on his meta-analysis of research findings, Falloon and colleagues (1998) conclude that appropriate medication can decrease symptoms in 75 percent of individuals with schizophrenia, reducing their risk of relapse from 70 percent to 30 to 40 percent. Medication can also increase the response of consumers to other interventions, such as social skills training. In spite of these potential benefits, studies have shown that up to 50 percent of individuals with a serious mental illness will be medication nonadherent within the first year; as many as 70 percent may be nonadherent within two years (Jamison, 1997; Weiden, Olfson, and Essock, 1997).

For many individuals, medication serves as the foundation for their rehabilitation and allows them to manage their illness in the community. In contrast, consumers who discontinue medication on their own or do not take their medication as prescribed risk a recurrence of symptoms and ultimately a relapse. Medication nonadherence has many causes, including medication side effects, increased positive symptoms that interfere with treatment, and a poor relationship with members of the treatment team (Fenton, Blyler, and Heinssen, 1997). These and other sources of nonadherence are appropriate focuses of intervention.

Implications for Relapse Prevention. The vulnerability-stress model has important implications for relapse prevention. Initially, as consumers assume responsibility for managing their illness, they need to identify their symptoms, learn effective symptom management strategies, and monitor their symptoms for signs of impending relapse. Once they have identified their personal symptom triggers, they can avoid them or at least decrease their exposure.

Consumers can minimize their risk factors by developing good stress management skills, avoiding alcohol and street drugs, and maintaining regular eating and sleeping patterns. When increased exposure to a risk factor is unavoidable, such as the stress associated with a new job, they can anticipate and prepare for possible problems. Strengthening their protective factors, consumers can improve their prospects for recovery by following their medication regime, developing effective coping skills, and expanding their support network, perhaps by participating in a consumer support group or drop-in center. Finally, they need to identify personal warning signs that can signal an impending relapse. In fact, with time, most consumers and family members are able to identify these warning signs (Amenson, 1998a).

Nevertheless, some consumers can have little stress in their lives, take medication as prescribed, and avoid substance abuse—and still experience a relapse. In some cases, even the best treatment and the most cooperative consumer cannot avert a relapse. Although it is often the case that there is a precipitating event or a sequence of events, this is not always so. For some individuals, there is no clear explanation of why symptoms return or worsen; it may be that their medication simply stops working.

Relapse Prevention

The multifactorial process of relapse prevention requires knowledge of the stages of illness, recognition of the variables that may contribute to relapse for a given individual, availability of a support system in crisis situations, and development of a sensible plan of action agreed to by the consumer. As Amenson (1998a) has discussed, many variables can influence the risk of relapse, including illness variables (for example, history, symptoms, and treatment responsiveness), consumer variables (for example, prior level of functioning, personality style, acceptance of the illness, treatment adherence, coping strategies, and substance use), system variables (for example, service availability and adequacy), and family variables (for example, level of support and quality of family environment). A majority of these variables can be modified by an effective relapse-prevention plan.

Central to the relapse-prevention process is a careful assessment of the individual's symptoms, symptom triggers, risk factors, protective factors, and warning signs. This analysis of the individual's unique illness characteristics allows the practitioner to decide which elements of the relapse-prevention plan are most essential for that person. The plan typically includes psychosocial and pharmacological intervention, often in combination.

Psychosocial Intervention. Psychosocial treatment is an important tool in the prevention of relapse, although its effectiveness has only recently been documented in the literature. Results of early studies of psychosocial intervention were equivocal due to the nature of treatments studied and the absence of rigorous research methods (Mojtabai, Nicholson, and Carpenter, 1998). Recently, however, following their review of six controlled studies, Penn and Mueser (1996) concluded that psychosocial intervention results in significant improvement in behavioral functioning, as well as modest improvement in symptoms and community functioning. Potentially useful psychosocial interventions are consumer and family psychoeducation, social skills training, psychotherapy, community support, and lifestyle management.

Consumer and Family Psychoeducation. Psychoeducation is usually a necessary but not sufficient tool in relapse-prevention efforts. This intervention optimally has both consumer and family components. Consumer components typically include education about mental illness and its management, emphasis on medication adherence, and training in social skills. Family components usually include an empathic, validating, nonblaming, task-oriented alliance with the family; education about mental illness and its management; training in coping skills, such as communication, problem solving, and stress management; and social support, especially through contact with other families.

There is strong evidence that psychoeducation reduces the rate of relapse for consumers, as well as suggestive evidence that this intervention improves consumer functioning and family well-being. Education alone appears to be less effective than intervention that provides support, problem solving, and crisis intervention. Psychoeducational intervention of at least nine months' duration may be necessary to see effects, although some programs continue for a year or more (Dixon and Lehman, 1995).

Based on the empirical support for its effectiveness, interest is increasing in psychoeducation, which can be modified to meet the needs of particular providers, consumers, and families. For instance, psychoeducational programs can be offered to individual families or multifamily groups, and it can focus on specific diagnoses, such as schizophrenia or bipolar disorder (Miklowitz and Goldstein, 1997; Mueser and Glynn, 1999). On the other hand, psychoeducation is primarily provided by a professional team over a relatively long period, which may limit this intervention to certain settings.

When offering consumer psychoeducation, providers need to take into account any cognitive deficits that may be associated with the illness, such as limitations in concentration or short-term memory. Among the strategies that may enhance learning ability are frequent repetition of material, role-playing exercises, assignments, multiple modes of presentation (for example, both visual and auditory), and personal application of material. Such teaching strategies can increase the likelihood that what is taught will in fact be learned. The goal is to ensure that participants are able to understand, remember, and apply the material presented.

An additional problem is the failure to include the family component in psychoeducation. In fact, less than 10 percent of families with a member with schizophrenia receive educational and supportive services (Lehman, Steinwachs, and the Co-investigators of the PORT Project, 1998). Few mental health systems have the resources, and fewer clinicians have the training and experience, to offer ongoing psychoeducational programs. Yet the rationale for such services is strong: family psychoeducation has the potential to reduce relapse, improve treatment access and adherence, decrease family burden, and enhance social support for both consumer and family (Marsh, 1998). Clearly family services are cost-effective over the long term in reducing costly hospitalization.

Social Skills Training. Traditional treatment of serious mental illness has largely focused on symptom reduction through medication. However, the emphasis is increasing on rehabilitation services that can improve quality of life and promote recovery through enhanced skills, resources, and supports. Social skills training can assist consumers in improving their functioning in major domains of life and achieving their residential, educational, vocational, interpersonal, and recreational goals (Liberman and others, 1994). For instance, training might focus on skills that contribute to assertiveness, community and daily living, or friendship and conversation (Bellack, Mueser, Gingerich, and Agresta, 1997).

Psychotherapy. Psychotherapy can also be a useful tool in preventing relapse. However, this intervention is not indicated for all consumers with serious mental illness, nor are all forms of psychotherapy equally beneficial. Studies have shown that psychoanalytically oriented therapy designed to uncover unconscious processes is of little value when treating serious mental illness (Lehman and others, 1998). In contrast, other forms of therapy, such as cognitive therapy, may be useful in improving coping skills and mediating negative thought processes (Fowler, Garety, and Kuipers, 1995; Perris, 1989). In addition, Hogarty and colleagues (1995) have developed Personal Therapy, a psychotherapeutic procedure designed to help individuals progress through various stages in building a therapeutic relationship and in developing specific skills for managing the illness.

Community Support. A strong support system is needed for both maintaining individuals in the community and preventing relapse. The deinstitutionalization that occurred in the 1960s was supposed to result in a transition to community support for individuals who were discharged from institutions. In many cases, this did not occur. Indeed, few supports were available for those who were transferred to nursing homes, entered the correctional system, or joined the ranks of the homeless (Torrey, 1997). An effort is now under way to incorporate community support into programs for people with serious mental illness, drawing on both professional and natural support systems.

Community support is an essential component of a relapse prevention plan. Professional supports include ACT teams, such as those described by Stein (1993). These community-based teams offer multidisciplinary, twenty-four-hour support designed to maintain the individual in the community (Stein and Santos, 1997). Natural supports may include family, friends, or significant others in the consumer's life. Members of this natural support system can often benefit from education about mental illness, strategies for managing the illness, and suggestions for responding to a crisis.

Lifestyle Management. Lifestyle issues are an important focus of relapse-prevention efforts. Medication, consumer and family psychoeducation, social skills training, and community support can facilitate treatment, rehabilitation, and recovery. Lifestyle management helps to ensure that consumers maintain recovery. A healthy lifestyle includes a proper amount of sleep, appropriate dietary intake, a moderate exercise program, and a healthy balance of satisfying activities. Insufficient sleep or an inadequate diet are physiological and psychological stressors that can precipitate or be an early warning sign of relapse. In contrast, exercise serves to reduce stress, decrease depressive symptoms, and provide a physical release of energy.

Use of caffeine and cigarettes should be monitored, because both are nervous system stimulants that can potentiate anxiety symptoms. Lifestyle management plans should target alcohol and street drugs in light of the high incidence of a co-occurring substance disorder (Fowler, Carr, Carter, and Lewin, 1998). Integrated treatment programs are increasingly available for individuals who are dually diagnosed with a serious mental illness and a substance abuse problem. A referral can also be made to self-help groups specifically designed for those who have a dual diagnosis. Some of these groups use the twelve-step model popularized by Alcoholics Anonymous. Other programs use a harm-reduction model that does not require absolute abstinence, accepting consumers where they are in the recovery process.

Pharmacological Intervention. Medication often provides the foundation for a relapse-prevention plan. For many individuals, medication serves to alleviate or decrease symptoms and to facilitate participation in psychosocial programs. From the perspective of relapse prevention, however, two factors should be taken into account when evaluating medication usage. The first is the effect of the medication on the consumer: the efficacy of the medication, any side effects that may be occurring, and the consumer's attitude toward the medication. Good communication between the consumer and the treatment team is essential in assessing whether the medication is efficacious and in monitoring medication side effects.

In fact, the presence of side effects is one of the main reasons for medication nonadherence. Some side effects associated with psychotropic medication can be extremely debilitating or unpleasant, including muscle stiffness, akathisia (an inner sense of restlessness), and sexual dysfunction. Side effects are a predictable feature of pharmacotherapy. Thus, when medication is prescribed, providers should educate consumers and their caregivers about potential side effects and their management. For instance, consumers need to know which side effects require immediate attention, which they should mention at their next medication check, and which are likely to decrease with time and can be safely ignored.

The second medication factor is the adherence of the individual to the prescribed regime. Studies have indicated that a large number of individuals discontinue their medication without discussing this issue with their physician, often because they do not understand its role in the recovery process. Many consumers receive little information about their medication, its potential side effects, and the frequent need to take medication on an ongoing basis.

Persistent denial of the illness can also increase the likelihood of non-adherence; from the consumer's perspective, there is no need to treat an illness that does not exist. In addition, the feelings of anger and grief that are commonly experienced with long-term illnesses can increase the likelihood of nonadherence. When such feelings are present, the medication may serve as a symbol that the person has been labeled "abnormal" or "crazy" or has been diagnosed with an incurable and progressive illness. Given the stigma and misconceptions that surround mental illness, it is essential for providers to explore possible reasons for medication nonadherence with consumers and to involve them in developing any medication plan.

Developing a Relapse-Prevention Plan

Both research findings and clinical experience have demonstrated that relapse is often preventable. Once consumers have acquired the requisite knowledge and skills, they can be encouraged to engage in activities that are most likely to reduce the risk for relapse and to improve their quality of life. Essential to this goal is the development of an active relapse-prevention plan. Such a plan is not just a tool to be used in times of crisis. Rather, a relapse-prevention plan should be a living document that can be modified as circumstances change, thus providing a blueprint for managing one's life and illness through all phases.

It is imperative that the development of a relapse-prevention plan be a collaborative process between the consumer and the treatment team. Whenever possible, it is good practice to involve as well important members of the consumer's support system in the process. Particularly during crises, these support persons can assume essential roles and responsibilities. A relapse-prevention plan should have the following components:

- Short- and long-term goals
- Names and telephone numbers of key members of professional and natural support systems
- Roles and responsibilities of the consumer, members of the support system, and providers

- Strategies for maintaining wellness, strengthening the support system, and accessing community resources

Roles for Psychologists

Psychologists have rarely been seen as the health care professional of choice for individuals diagnosed with serious mental illness. In the past, many reasons deterred psychologists from working in this area, including professional identity and training, the prevalence of a narrow services model that focused largely on symptom control through medication, and an overemphasis on the deficits and limitations associated with the illness. Current developments are reversing this trend, including the increasing recognition of the potential for recovery and the greater emphasis on psychosocial services that can improve quality of life.

These developments have generated expanding opportunities for psychologists to work in the area of serious mental illness. As practitioners, they can assist consumers to realize their potential as unique human beings who are not defined by their illness, help them learn to cope with the personal and social limitations associated with the illness, and support them in achieving meaningful, satisfying, and productive lives in their communities. As key members of the professional support system, psychologists can offer hope and encourage self-determination, key elements in the recovery process.

Treatment for serious mental illness has increasingly moved toward a team approach that benefits from the unique skills of each discipline, as well as the participation of consumers and their families. Psychologists can contribute significantly as leaders or members of the treatment team, taking a more active role than is traditionally encouraged in training programs. For instance, they can provide consumer and family psychoeducation about serious mental illness, offer social skills training designed to enhance vocational and interpersonal functioning, assist consumers to expand their support network, help them maintain a healthy lifestyle, and offer individual psychotherapy that can help them reclaim and rebuild their lives. In other roles, psychologists can educate paraprofessional members of the treatment team and serve as members of the ACT team.

In particular, the new emphasis on relapse prevention in serious mental illness offers psychologists new opportunities and roles for which they are uniquely suited. Relapse-prevention programs are empirically supported, competency based, and skills oriented, an approach consistent with psychological training and practice. Assuming leadership roles, psychologists can work with consumers and members of their support network to develop individualized relapse-prevention plans. For example, they can assist consumers in the following ways:

- Assuming an assertive and informed role in treatment and rehabilitation
- Identifying, monitoring, and managing their symptoms

- Identifying and avoiding their personal symptom triggers
- Identifying and minimizing their personal risk factors
- Identifying and strengthening their personal protective factors
- Understanding the role of medication in treatment
- Recognizing and responding to the warning signs of impending relapse
- Improving their stress management, assertiveness, problem solving, and communication skills
- Expanding their support network
- Improving their interpersonal skills and relationships
- Achieving their educational and vocational goals
- Developing an action plan for dealing with crises
- Conducting a relapse drill with key members of their support system
- Maintaining wellness by developing a healthy lifestyle
- Contributing their talents and gifts to society

References

Amenson, C. S. *Family Skills in Relapse Prevention.* Pasadena, Calif.: Pacific Clinics Institute, 1998a.

Amenson, C. S. *Schizophrenia: A Family Education Curriculum.* Pasadena, Calif.: Pacific Clinics Institute, 1998b.

Bellack, A. S., Mueser, K. T., Gingerich, S., and Agresta, J. *Social Skills Training for Schizophrenia: A Step-by-Step Guide.* New York: Guilford Press, 1997.

Dixon, L. B., and Lehman, A. F. "Family Interventions for Schizophrenia." *Schizophrenia Bulletin,* 1995, *21*(4), 631–643.

Falloon, I., Roncone, R., Malm, U., and Coverdale, J. "Effective and Efficient Treatment Strategies to Enhance Recovery from Schizophrenia: How Much Longer Will People Have to Wait Before We Provide Them." *Psychiatric Rehabilitation Skills,* 1998, *2*(2), 107–127.

Fenton, W. S., Blyler, C. R., and Heinssen, R. K. "Determinants of Medication Compliance in Schizophrenia: Empirical and Clinical Findings." *Schizophrenia Bulletin,* 1997, *23*(4), 637–651.

Fowler, D., Garety, P., and Kuipers, E. *Cognitive Therapy for Psychosis: Theory and Practice.* New York: Wiley, 1995.

Fowler, I. L., Carr, V. J., Carter, N. T., and Lewin, T. J. "Patterns of Current and Lifetime Substance Use in Schizophrenia." *Schizophrenia Bulletin,* 1998, *24*(3), 443–455.

Green, R. S., and Rabiner, C. J. "Making Rehospitalization Part of the Plan." *Hospital and Community Psychiatry,* 1978, *29*(1), 36–37.

Harding, C. M., Zubin, J., and Strauss, J. S. "Chronicity in Schizophrenia: Revisited." *British Journal of Psychiatry,* 1992, *161*(Suppl. 18), 27–37.

Hogarty, G. E., and others. "Personal Therapy: A Disorder-Relevant Psychotherapy for Schizophrenia." *Schizophrenia Bulletin,* 1995, *21*(3), 379–392.

Jamison, K. R. "Lithium Compliance in Manic-Depressive Illness." In B. Blackwell (ed.), *Treatment Compliance and the Therapeutic Alliance.* Newark, N.J.: Harwood Academic, 1997.

Lehman, A. F., Steinwachs, D. M., and the Co-investigators of the PORT Project. "At Issue: Translating Research into Practice: The Schizophrenia Patient Outcomes Research Team (PORT) Treatment Recommendations." *Schizophrenia Bulletin,* 1998, *24*(1),1–10.

Liberman, R. P., and others. "Skills Training for the Seriously Mentally Ill: Modules in the UCLA Social and Independent Living Skills Program." In R. J. Ancill, S. Holliday, and J. Higenbottam (eds.), *Schizophrenia: Exploring the Spectrum of Psychosis.* New York: Wiley, 1994.

Marsh, D. T. *Serious Mental Illness and the Family: The Practitioner's Guide.* New York: Wiley, 1998.

Miklowitz, D. J., and Goldstein, M. J. *Bipolar Disorder: A Family-Focused Treatment Approach.* New York: Guilford Press, 1997.

Mojtabai, R., Nicholson, R. A., and Carpenter, B. N. "Role of Psychosocial Treatments in Management of Schizophrenia: A Meta-analytic Review of Controlled Studies." *Schizophrenia Bulletin,* 1998, 24(4), 569–587.

Moller, M. D., and Murphy, M. F. "The Three R's Rehabilitation Program: A Prevention Approach for the Management of Relapse Symptoms Associated with Psychiatric Diagnoses." *Psychiatric Rehabilitation Journal,* 1997, 20(3), 42–48.

Mueser, K. T., Drake, R. E., and Wallach, M. A. "Dual Diagnosis: A Review of Etiological Theories." *Addictive Behaviors,* 1998, 23(6), 717–734.

Mueser, K. T., and Glynn, S. M. *Behavioral Family Therapy for Psychiatric Disorders.* (2nd ed.) Oakland, Calif.: New Harbinger, 1999.

Penn, D. L., and Mueser, K. T. "Research Update on the Psychosocial Treatment of Schizophrenia." *American Journal of Psychiatry,* 1996, 153(5), 607–617.

Perris, C. *Cognitive Therapy with Schizophrenic Patients.* New York: Guilford Press, 1989.

Regier, D. A., and others. "Comorbidity of Mental Disorders with Alcohol and Other Drug Abuse: Results from the Epidemiologic Catchment Area (ECA) Study." *Journal of the American Medical Association,* 1990, 264(19), 2511–2518.

Stein, L. "A System Approach to Reducing Relapse in Schizophrenia." *Journal of Clinical Psychiatry,* 1993, 54 (3 suppl.), 7–12.

Stein, L. I., and Santos, A. B. *Assertive Community Treatment of Persons with Severe Mental Illness.* New York: Norton, 1997.

Steinberg, J. R. "Substance Abuse and Psychosis." In R. J. Ancill, S. Holliday, and J. Higenbottam (eds.), *Schizophrenia: Exploring the Spectrum of Psychosis.* New York: Wiley, 1994.

Torrey, E. F. *Surviving Schizophrenia: A Manual for Families, Consumers and Providers.* (3rd ed.) New York: HarperCollins, 1995.

Torrey, E. F. *Out of the Shadows: Confronting America's Mental Illness Crisis.* New York: Wiley, 1997.

Wasylenki, D. A. "Psychotherapy of Schizophrenia Revisited." *Hospital and Community Psychiatry,* 1992, 43(2), 123–127.

Weiden, P., Olfson, M., and Essock, S. "Medication Non-Compliance in Schizophrenia: Effects on Mental Health Service Policy." In B. Blackwell (ed.), *Treatment Compliance and the Therapeutic Alliance.* Newark, N.J.: Harwood Academic, 1997.

DAVID P. WALLING *is associated with InfoScriber Corporation.*

DIANE T. MARSH *is professor of psychology at the University of Pittsburgh at Greensburg.*

6

Focusing on a variety of relevant psychological theories, this chapter addresses important elements in the recovery process for people with serious mental disabilities.

A Psychological View of People with Serious Mental Illness

Robert D. Coursey, Jean Gearon, Mary A. Bradmiller, Jennifer Ritsher, Andy Keller, Peter Selby

In order to make sense out of our experiences, we tend to perceive the "unknown out there" through the lens of what we already know or believe. In the area of mental illness, some people use the lens of the medical model with its categorical diagnoses and biological perspectives in interpreting the behavior and expressions of people with severe mental illnesses. Others use the fear-based "stigma" lens of ridicule and rejection. Still others view people with these problems from a spiritual or religious view. We are usually unaware of our own lenses and therefore do not see the need for their correction.

For many of us, the breakthrough event in this sorry and often destructive history of distorted perceptions was the large-scale availability of first-person accounts from people who have been diagnosed as having schizophrenia or other disabling psychiatric diagnoses. The humanity of those who are struggling against great odds begins to dissolve the distortions in the lens. Moreover, these first-person accounts offer therapists, researchers, and other consumers a large catalogue of helpful interventions.

In this chapter we merge consumers' views with psychological theory and research. We believe that a psychological perspective with its empirically supported information on coping, resilience, competence, optimism, and other relevant concepts can provide useful insights, interventions, and theory for both consumers and service providers. Our focus does not negate or disregard the biological; the two play integrated complementary roles. (We have addressed the integration of biology and psychology in Coursey, 1994, and Coursey, Alford, and Safarjan, 1997.)

We present some alternative approaches to understanding and organizing interventions for people with disabling psychiatric disorders. Our research team at the University of Maryland at College Park has explored a number of ways to understand these disorders in collaboration with considerable consumer input throughout the research projects. We have consciously relied on a series of assumptions, concepts, and methodologies common to psychological theories and methodologies. Our goal was to try out a variety of psychological concepts and methods that seemed promising to help us better understand the human experiences of these states along with efforts to improve lives.

This article explores three areas:

The competency model based on the early work of Jahoda (1958), Garmezy (1983), Tyler (1978), Wright (1960, 1983), and more recent work by Glantz and Johnson (1999), Higgins (1994), and Tyler (1991). These researchers primarily worked with disadvantaged youth and adults who faced overwhelming odds but were consistently able to achieve their goals

The Acceptance of Disability model developed by Dembo, Leviton, and Wright (1956) and White (1959) for people with physical disabilities

Theories and research about gender differences that are rich veins to mine, but seldom applied to people with psychiatric disabilities

Competency and Coping

In the late 1980s, we decided to stop looking at psychopathology and to think about its opposite: growth, health, competencies, and the common humanity of us all. Over a year's time, we made a basic decision: to build on the psychological theory and research in competency. Its literature provided us with a basic model that we suspected could be extended to those who were able to deal so effectively with severe mental disabilities. We were fortunate enough to develop friendships and working relations with a group of very impressive people with severe mental disabilities who helped us in all aspects of our research.

Our exploration of the literature, discussions, and the results of the competency and resilience research led us to six critical characteristics that clarified the differences between highly competent copers and average copers among people diagnosed with schizophrenia (for a complete description of the methodology and outcomes, see Gearon, 1995):

- Clients' attitudes toward the disability
- A framework for understanding the disability
- Coping strategies
- Perceived self-competency
- Social support
- Turning points on the road to recovery

Clients' Attitudes Toward the Disability. Highly competent consumers thought that the diagnosis provided a framework for understanding the illness, which in turn informed their coping and led to medication use. They also felt that the diagnosis was stigmatizing. Competent clients said that their medication helped alleviate their psychotic symptoms and allowed them to function more effectively; the average coper reported that it reduced their anxiety and that they were just following the doctor's orders. The highly competent volunteers seemed more reflective, and we wondered whether they were also more responsive to their medication. They also saw relapse as a temporary event that one just has to accept and as an opportunity for growth. The average clients had few or no responses about relapses. The highly competent clients thus seemed more able to roll with the punches and were reflective and optimistic.

Clients' Framework for Understanding the Disability. The whole sample provided a wide variety of expected responses about the causes of their problem, such as biology, stress, family, and drugs and alcohol. The only difference was that the average copers gave "me" as a cause twice as much as the high-competency clients did. In asking whether their theory of the cause helped them to think about their problem, twice the number of high-competency clients mentioned ways it helped (for example, "It leads to a coping strategy," "It provides a framework to understand it," and "It relieves guilt"). The average coper thus seemed to accept the blame for failure more often than the high-competency clients did.

Coping Strategies. Across a variety of situations, competent copers were more proactive in coping. They identified more coping strategies and especially more proactive ones, such as talking with others, using relaxation techniques, and reducing stress through exercise. The competent copers also reported making treatment choices. In answering what was least helpful, significantly more competent clients responded, "The lack of the right kind of understanding."

We also asked how they coped specifically with their mental illness when their symptoms returned. A great variety of responses fell into ten categories, including talking with others, reducing stress in various ways, getting active, praying, contacting mental health professionals, and medication. All of the highly competent clients had one or more way to cope. When we asked about dealing with problems in their housing, 57 percent of the competent clients named an active attempt to solve the problem; none gave a passive strategy.

Almost all of the highly competent folks made choices in their treatment and said this involvement gave them a feeling of control and facilitated growth; only 10 percent of the average clients had this response.

The lack of any coping skills to deal with the return of the symptoms could signify a failure of the staff in developing and training everyone in coping techniques. Also, the difference may be due to differences in cognitive function and recall, in generating ideas, or in IQ.

Perceived Self-Competency. Three-fourths of the highly competent clients felt competent in helping others, setting and achieving personal and career goals, developing personal relationships, and being a leader and role model; less than half of the average group felt so. Most interesting was the answer to the question of whether the client had always been an effective coper. Only 12 percent of the high group but 60 percent of the average group said yes. It is likely that the effective copers had made clear growth, while the average coper had not changed much.

When asked how they contributed to developing their own competency, the high achievers said that they required themselves to function like other adults, putting themselves in challenging situations, and "never giving up on myself." On the other hand, some of the average but none of the high-competency persons said, "By taking my medication."

Social Support. Almost everyone we asked said that they had active support from their family, but there were interesting differences. A slightly higher percentage of the high-competency clients reported more emotional and instrumental support. Average clients reported family help with monitoring medication and symptoms, while none of the high group did; but almost all highly competent clients actively sought support from their family versus lower levels on the part of the average clients. Replicating results from other studies, the high-competency clients reported that encouragement and understanding from staff were most helpful, while the average client identified practical advice as the most helpful. This finding has been replicated in another study on psychotherapy with people with severe mental illness (Coursey, Keller, and Farrell, 1995).

We looked at various other aspects of social support. For instance, when we asked about best friends, we found that more high-competency clients had supportive best friends, had a role model with mental illness, and had someone who would push and challenge them yet never push their own agenda or use abusive and critical pushing. Also, more high-competency clients gave support to others, helped others, and provided peer support. Finally, this group gave less material support such as loaning money or buying cigarettes for others.

Turning Points on the Road to Recovery. Ninety-six percent of the highly competent clients had experienced a powerful turning point that had set them on the road to recovery. Two-thirds of the average competent clients also had experienced a turning point. Here, too, qualitative differences were seen. For the highly competent clients, the turning point provided an education about their illness and living skills that helped the clients to be responsible. For some, it hooked them up with a support group, caused a change in attitude about the future, and gave them hope. A common turning point was obtaining housing, which reduced their stress and gave them a sense of normality. They no longer felt alone.

Follow-up Work. We have recently followed up on this work in our research team in several ways. Howard (1999) has developed an assessment instrument to measure this competence, Lee (1998) has investigated Lazarus's coping style (and found that it is not very reliable and useful for people with serious mental disabilities), and Lucksted (1997) has completed an in-depth qualitative study of turning points.

Implications. These six dimensions of competencies go beyond a simple coping concept. All have a developmental process, and all but the last one are modifiable through psychological interventions. We have not yet adequately confronted the issue of neuropsychological deficits in the model. For instance, Dickinson (2000) has recently shown that basic information processing variables such as working memory and processing speed from the Wechsler Adult Intelligent Scale III are important in understanding how well people function in the community. Fortunately, psychologists (Green, 1998; Corrigan and Yudofsy, 1996) are beginning to figure out how to change these deficits with behavioral and psychological interventions.

Acceptance of Disabilities

The competency model was originally developed with disadvantaged persons who faced great difficulties. What the competency model lacks is a dimension that focuses on disability. While research clinicians are beginning to learn how to improve the functioning of people with cognitive and other disabilities such as negative symptoms, it is important to provide a psychological approach for clients struggling to come to terms with mental disabilities. Such an approach has been developed that can be used with persons who have disabilities due to their mental illness.

The Acceptance of Disability model (Dembo and others, 1956; Wright, 1960, 1983) focuses on four value changes that are very helpful for people with disabilities: (1) awakening to new possibilities in life, (2) knowing that a person is more than his or her mental illness, (3) devaluing lost abilities and resolving grief, and (4) valuing the self without using social comparison. We explored the applicability of this physical disability model by developing a parallel Acceptance of Psychiatric Disability scale that demonstrated construct validity by correlating with most of the same measures that correlated with the original Acceptance of Disability scale (Linkowski, 1969). We administered the psychiatric disability scale to 111 people (59 males and 52 females) who had long-term mental illnesses and attended psychiatric rehabilitation centers. First, we asked whether they identified as having a mental illness. Twenty-four percent ($n = 27$) reported using other explanations for their symptoms. For those 76 percent identifying as mentally ill, the scores on the Acceptance of Psychiatric Disability scale positively correlated with self-esteem, education, and positive attitudes toward physically disabled people. It also correlated negatively with anxiety and external locus of control. Acceptance of disability for people who have mental illness was not related to the duration of the disability and was negatively correlated to symptom severity.

The study also demonstrated that people with serious mental illness successfully came to terms with their situation by use of other lenses, including conceptualizing themselves as persons with a physical illness such as epilepsy, as survivors of childhood trauma, as members of an oppressed group, and as having a drug problem. This group of participants had favorable levels of self-esteem, quality of life, and symptom severity roughly equivalent to those who believed they had a mental illness and were high on acceptance of this disability. The study researchers suggested that service providers might do well to discover and work within their clients' lenses or metaphors rather than subscribing only to formal diagnoses according to the *Diagnostic and Statistical Manual of Mental Disorders.* Overall this work supports the importance of consumers' coming to terms with their disabilities in a positive and constructive manner. It also suggests that the acceptance of disability is an important construct that should be included in a psychological model of recovery.

Gender Issues

Traditionally mental health services have focused on the psychopathological aspect of the client's functioning and have largely ignored the gendered aspect of the clients. This was especially true because most research was done with men. Fortunately, this incredible oversight is being corrected (Ritsher, Coursey, and Farrell, 1997; Seeman, 1995; Weissman and Riba, 1995). Although there is now some new interest in learning about women with severe mental illnesses, the gender aspect of men with severe disabilities has similarly been ignored. We briefly describe the results of three studies focusing on gender (Ritsher, Coursey, and Farrell, 1997; Keller, 1994; Selby, 1995).

Women and Serious Mental Illness. The feminist literature suggests that women in general have quite different socialization experiences than do men, and these result in different characteristic strengths and weaknesses (Jordan and others, 1991; Miller, 1984; Seeman, 1995). For this study, we chose and drew on relational theory, as developed by Miller and her colleagues at the Stone Center of Wellesley College. According to Jordan and Miller (Jordan and others, 1991; Miller, 1988), a satisfying relationship is the central source of empowering energy and psychological growth for women. If the relationship is not satisfying and the woman feels a sense of psychological disconnection from her partner, the results are psychological turmoil and a corrosion of self-worth and identity. More specifically, relational theory posits that when a woman experiences mutual, validating relationships, she will have more "relational zest," a greater range of competencies, a more complex sense of self, and a greater sense of self-worth. If a woman instead feels shut off or disconnected from others, she will not only lack the benefits of an empowering relationship, but will be psychologically weakened and made vulnerable by the sense of disconnection that she feels.

If relational theory can be meaningfully applied to women with serious mental illness, relationships should be more central to them than to men with serious mental illness, and the impact of relationships on women's identity and experience should not be completely obscured by the impact of the illness. In fact, some empirical evidence supports the relationship orientation of women with severe mental illness. For example, women with schizophrenia tend to have better premorbid social competence and better social networks than do men (Zigler, Levine, and Zigler, 1977).

Self-Understandings of Mental Illness. In this study, the views of 107 women receiving services in psychiatric rehabilitation centers were compared with the views of men (*n* = 59) from the same centers. All differences reported here were significant at the .05 percent level. As with many other surveys we have done, most clients knew what their diagnosis was, but about 40 percent of both women and men did not believe that they had a mental illness. When we asked how they explained their illness to themselves, twice as many women than men (45 percent versus 23 percent) said that bad things had happened to them in the past or that it was the result of the way they were raised (24 percent versus 6 percent). Their views certainly conform to feminist assertions that trauma is an important contributor to women's mental illness. A growing set of research confirms the role of violence in serious mental illness (Mueser and others, 1998).

Formative Life Experiences. When we asked our sample what were their memorable life events, 48 percent of the women mentioned relationship issues or becoming a parent versus 13 percent for the men. On the other hand, 41 percent of the men (versus 20 percent of the women) identified work, accomplishments, and striving. Evidently traditional roles and values of women with serious mental illness are similar to the population at large.

Two-thirds of both women and men reported physical abuse. However, when we asked about sexual abuse, 57 percent of the women and 30 percent of the men reported sexual abuse. When asked about physical and sexual abuse from service providers, 2 to 7 percent of women replied that it had occurred. On average it took place fifteen years ago. When asked how they responded to unwanted sex, both women and men said they usually could say no 30 to 40 percent of the time. Most interestingly, only 3 percent of the women reported that they could never say no, while 13 percent of the males could never say no.

Personal Relationships. Feminist thought emphasizes the importance of personal relationships in women. Women with serious mental illness resoundingly affirmed this. From having a best friend, to asking for and giving help, to having a pet, to a long-term romantic partner, twice as many women as men reported yes. As expected, women reared more children, lived with or were in contact with their children, and reported that their illness made it harder for them to be good parents. (See Chapter 7 of this issue.) Two to four times more women were involved in these relationship activities than men. Finally, 19 percent of the women and 30 percent of the men reported that they were lesbian, gay, or bisexual. If these percentages are replicated elsewhere, programs need to be developed for this group.

Professional Relationships and Services. Stories of abuse and poor relationships with staff are quite common. Our results on women's view of their relationships with therapists and staff did not refute its occurrence, but did suggest that it might be less prevalent than the literature suggests. Over three-quarters of the women respondents affirmed that both their therapists and staff made them feel respected or like an equal, 61 percent said it was not difficult to disagree with them, 85 percent said that their physicians took them seriously when they talked about physical symptoms, and 70 percent reported they received regular breast and pelvic exams and birth control care. Only 4 percent felt treated like a child. Of course, these responses will vary across service programs, and even the best programs can be improved.

Impact of Illness. Thirty-seven percent of the women felt a loss of femininity due to the illness, and about 50 percent reported having to give up or change important life goals. In terms of their general life satisfaction, 16 percent were very dissatisfied, 30 percent were between dissatisfied and satisfied, and 54 percent reported being very or completely satisfied. These are quite low percentages for life satisfaction surveys.

Summary of Findings. In summary, women with severe mental disabilities seem to reflect the major characteristics of women without mental illness, and their life events are congruent with the views of moderate feminists. These findings seem quite relevant for developing gender-specific services and interventions for women.

Men and Serious Mental Illness. The first study of men (Keller, 1994) used a series of nine focus groups to explore the masculine beliefs of males with serious mental disabilities. Using the iterative case method of Strauss and Corbin (1990), sixty-four men from four psychosocial rehabilitation centers generated and discussed their list of masculine beliefs. The same process occurred in each new group until no new beliefs were generated. The participants in each group rated how important their set of beliefs was "in order to be a man." A final taxonomy of seventy-eight masculine beliefs from all of the focus groups was developed by a team of researchers in a careful iterative (Eisenhardt, 1989) and content-analytic method (Schneider, Wheeler, and Cox, 1992). Four major masculine beliefs emerged:

Responsibility: "A man takes on responsibilities" and "succeeds at what he does."
Independence: A man "is self-reliant" and "is able to access support."
Strength: A man "has interpersonal, emotional, mental, physical and character strength."
Interpersonal relationships: A man "has relationships with other men, with family and kids, is sexual, and is influenced by his father."

These masculine beliefs are what might be expected of adult males, but they raised our concerns about the impact of "not measuring up" to "being a man" on their self-esteem, level of depression, and symptoms.

In the next study (Selby, 1995), we addressed the relationship between living up to their masculinity beliefs and their psychological adjustment. Using the previous taxonomy of seventy-eight items, we developed forty-seven items for a new measure of masculine attributes. Two hundred thirty-eight men with serious mental illness rated each of the forty-seven beliefs in terms of "how much like me" and "how important each item was to being a man." They also filled out measures of psychiatric symptoms and adjustment: the Brief Symptom Inventory, Beck Depression Inventory, the Rosenberg Self-Esteem Scale, the Self-Efficacy Scale, and the Internalized Shame Scale. The forty-seven-item scale was reliable. A factor analysis yielded three main, stable factors:

Morality, which included items such as "kind to others," "does a good job," "lives by his values," "defends his beliefs," and "is spiritual"
Family values, which included "takes care of his family," "has a wife or girl-friend," "the breadwinner," "takes care of a family or girlfriend"
Toughness, which included items such as "controls his emotions, his anger," "physically strong," "plays sports," and "has strength to endure hardships"

We developed a personal discrepancy score between the strength of a man's beliefs ("how important each item was to being a man") versus how well he implements that value in his life ("how much like me"). We then examined whether this difference between the importance of their gender ideals and their inability to live out their values was correlated with their psychological health.

We found that the greater the discrepancy was between these men's ideal masculine beliefs versus their evaluation of how well they conformed to their masculinity beliefs correlated negatively with a variety of symptom measures. The greater the discrepancy was, the more the depression ($r = .32$), the higher their global symptom severity ($r = .21$), the more of their internalized shame ($r = .26$), and the lower their self-efficacy beliefs ($r = .33$).

These three studies make clear that gender issues, whether abusive relationships or the lack of a comforting companion, or the inability to measure up to one's masculine beliefs, are important therapeutic issues for recovery. They need to be taken into account in the same way that culture, jobs, housing, stigma (Link and others, 1997), and other significant psychosocial issues affect the welfare and outcomes of people with psychiatric disabilities.

Conclusion

In order to develop a basic psychological framework for understanding people with psychiatric disabilities, we have attempted to work closely with consumers to ensure that the model is consistent with their experiences. The elements of this competency framework currently include attitudes toward disability, clients' framework for understanding the disability, coping strategies, a sense of self-efficacy or self-competency, social support, and turning points. To this we added the Acceptance of Disability model with its four values. We also explored the importance of gender in understanding people with psychiatric disabilities. Beyond that, we did not discuss the role of other sociodemographics of people with long-term disabilities. We are continuing to explore other potential psychological components such as optimism.

However well developed the competency model may become, questions will still remain. For instance, how do we construe the interface between competencies that people have and the psychological, behavioral, and biological interventions (Scott and Dixon, 1995; Drury, Birchwood, Cochrane, and MacMillan, 1996) that are provided to them? There is a great need for better theoretical and practical frameworks.

There are other significant psychological perspectives on consumer development, especially the psychological notion of recovery. This area is rich with ideas, attitudes, coping, and other elements (Anthony, 1993; Spaniol, Gagne, and Koehler, 1997). The exploding range of coping strategies has spilled over to family members and providers alike (Mueser and Gingerich, 1994; Hatfield and Lefley, 1993). This coping approach, however, lacks a strong conceptual organization, focuses more on the process than on structure, and does not yet have much empirical validation. With the explosion of information that it has generated, there is a need to develop a schema for understanding the various types of coping, when and where they are useful, what the dangers are, what their efficacy is, and what the best way is for consumers to learn them.

A critical missing component is the integration of the psychological with the biological. Although that might appear to undermine the psychological lenses, in fact, it would enhance it. There is a critical need for a holistic integration of all of the major factors. After all, the psychological and the biological are not parallel dimensions. We are ourselves mutually interacting systems embedded in even larger systems (Coursey, Alford, and Safarjan, 1997).

To return to our starting point, there are ways for all of us to develop better lenses to understand these phenomena. We need to raise the consciousness of society about the distorting lenses that society wears, and we need improved lenses for the care providers as well as the consumers themselves who are not exempt from biases and distortions. But the most powerful force for change is exposure to people with psychiatric disabilities.

References

Anthony, W. "Recovery from Mental Illness: The Guiding Vision of the Mental Health Service System in the 1990s." *Psychosocial Rehabilitation Journal*, 1993, *16*, 11–23.

Corrigan, P., and Yudofsy, S. *Cognitive Rehabilitation of Neuropsychiatric Disorders*. Washington, D.C.: American Psychiatric Press, 1996.

Coursey, R. D. "Serious Mental Illness: The Paradigm Shift Involved in Providing Services and Training Students." In D. T. Marsh (ed.), *New Directions in the Psychological Treatment of Serious Mental Illness*. New York: Praeger, 1994.

Coursey, R. D., Alford, J., and Safarjan, W. "Significant Advances in Understanding and Treating Serious Mental Illness." *Professional Psychology: Research and Practice*, 1997, *28*, 205–216.

Coursey, R. D., Keller, A. B., and Farrell, E. "Individual Psychotherapy and Persons with Serious Mental Illness: The Clients' Perspective." *Schizophrenia Bulletin*, 1995, *21*, 283–301.

Dembo, T., Leviton, G. H., and Wright, B. A. "Adjustment to Misfortune—A Problem in Social-Psychological Rehabilitation." *Artificial Limbs*, 1956, *3*, 4–62.

Dickinson, D. "Exploring WAIS III Variables in Everyday Functioning Among Individuals with Schizophrenia Spectrum Disorders." Unpublished doctoral dissertation, University of Maryland, 2000.

Drury, V., Birchwood, M., Cochrane, R., and MacMillan, F. "Cognitive Therapy and Recovery from Acute Psychosis: A Controlled Trial. I. Impact on Psychotic Symptoms." *British Journal of Psychiatry*, 1996, *169*, 593–601.

Eisenhardt, K. M. "Building Theories from Case Study Research." *Academy of Management Review*, 1989, *14*, 532–550.

Garmezy, N. "Stressors of Childhood." In N. Garmezy and M. Rutter (eds.), *Stress, Coping and Development in Children*. New York: McGraw-Hill, 1983.

Gearon, J. S. "An Exploratory Study of Competency and Good Mental Health in People with Schizophrenia." Unpublished doctoral dissertation, University of Maryland, 1995.

Glantz, M. D., and Johnson, J. L. *Resilience and Development: Positive Life Adaptations*. New York: Kluwer Academic, 1999.

Green, M. F. *Schizophrenia from a Neurocognitive Perspective*. Needham Heights, Mass.: Allyn and Bacon, 1998.

Hatfield, A. B., and Lefley, H. P. *Surviving Mental Illness: Stress, Coping, and Adaptation*. New York: Guilford Press, 1993.

Higgins, G. O. *Resilient Adults*. San Francisco: Jossey-Bass, 1994.

Howard, C. R. "Psychological, Social, and Coping Resources: A Tripartite Model of Competency in People with Serious Mental Illness." Unpublished master's thesis, University of Maryland, 1999.

Jahoda, N. *Current Concepts of Positive Mental Health*. New York: Basic Books, 1958.

Jordan, J. V., and others. *Women's Growth in Connection: Writings from the Stone Center*. New York: Guilford Press, 1991.

Keller, A. B. "Men with Serious Mental Illnesses and Their Masculine Beliefs." Unpublished doctoral dissertation, University of Maryland, 1994.

Lee, S. "A Study of People with Schizophrenia Who Are Exemplary and Average in Coping, Using Lazarus' Model of Coping." Unpublished Masters' thesis, University of Maryland, 1998.

Link, B. G., and others. "On Stigma and Its Consequences: Evidence from a Longitudinal Study of Men with Dual Diagnoses of Mental Illness and Substance Abuse." *Journal of Health and Social Behaviors*, 1997, *38*, 177–190.

Linkowski, D. C. "A Study of the Relationship Between Acceptance of Disability and Response to Rehabilitation." Unpublished doctoral dissertation, State University of New York, 1969.

Lucksted, A. A. "Empowerment and Positive Turning Points in the Lives of People with Serious Mental Illnesses." Unpublished doctoral dissertation, University of Maryland, 1997.

Miller, J. B. "The Development of Women's Sense of Self." Work in Progress, No. 33. Wellesley, Mass.: Stone Center Working Paper Series, 1984.

Miller, J. B. "Connections, Disconnections, and Violations." Work in Progress, No. 33. Wellesley, Mass.: Stone Center Working Paper Series, 1988.

Mueser, K. T., and Gingerich, S. *Coping with Schizophrenia*. Oakland, Calif.: New Harbinger Publications, 1994.

Mueser, K. T., and others. "Trauma and Posttraumatic Stress Disorder in Severe Mental Illness." *Journal of Consulting and Clinical Psychology*, 1998, *66*, 493–499.

Ritsher, J.E.B., Coursey, R. D., and Farrell, E. W. "A Survey on Issues in the Lives of Women with Severe Mental Illness." *Psychiatric Services*, 1997, *48*, 1273–1282.

Schneider, B., Wheeler, J. K., and Cox, J. F. "A Passion for Service: Using Content Analysis to Explicate Service Climate Themes." *Journal of Applied Psychology*, 1992, *77*, 705–716.

Scott, S. E., and Dixon, L. B. "Psychological Interventions for Schizophrenia." *Schizophrenia Bulletin,* 1995, *21,* 621–630.

Seeman, M. V. *Gender and Psychopathology.* Washington, D.C.: American Psychiatric Press, 1995.

Selby, P. M. "Gender Identity and Psychological Adjustment in Men with Serious Mental Illness." Unpublished doctoral dissertation, University of Maryland, 1995.

Spaniol, L., Gagne, C., and Koehler, M. (eds.). *Psychological and Social Aspects of Psychiatric Disability.* Boston: Center for Psychiatric Rehabilitation, Boston University, 1997.

Spaniol, L., and Koehler, M. *The Experience of Recovery.* Boston: Center for Psychiatric Rehabilitation, Boston University, 1995.

Strauss, A., and Corbin, J. *Basics of Qualitative Research.* Thousand Oaks, Calif.: Sage, 1990.

Tyler, F. B. "Individual Psychosocial Competence: A Personality Configuration." *Education and Psychological Measurements,* 1978, *38,* 209–323.

Tyler, F. B., Brome, D. R., and Williams, J. E. *Ethnic Validity, Ecology, and Psychotherapy: A Psychosocial Competence Model.* New York: Plenum, 1991.

Weissman, M. M., and Riba, M. B. "Psychiatric Disorders in Women and Women's Health Care." In J. M. Oldham and M. B. Riba (eds.), *Review of Psychiatry.* Washington, D.C.: American Psychiatric Press, 1995.

White, R. W. "Motivation Reconsidered: The Concept of Competence." *Psychological Review,* 1959, *66,* 297–333.

Wright, B. A. *Physical Disability: A Psychological Approach.* New York: HarperCollins, 1960.

Wright, B. A. *Physical Disability: A Psychosocial Approach.* New York: HarperCollins, 1983.

Zigler, E., Levine, J., and Zigler, B. "Premorbid Social Competence and Paranoid-Nonparanoid Status in Female Schizophrenic Patients." *Journal of Nervous and Mental Disease,* 1977, *164,* 333–339.

ROBERT D. COURSEY *is professor of clinical psychology at the University of Maryland at College Park, where he teaches and co-leads a graduate training program on serious mental illness.*

JEAN GEARON *is assistant professor in the Psychiatry Department in the School of Medicine at the University of Maryland at Baltimore. She does research on women with schizophrenia and trauma.*

MARY A. BRADMILLER *works in a mental health clinic in Minneapolis, Minnesota.*

JENNIFER RITSHER *works at the Center for Healthcare Evaluations at the Palo Alto VA/Stanford Medical School in Palo Alto, California.*

ANDY KELLER *is a consultant and executive of the Triwest Group, which develops programs for public mental health systems.*

PETER SELBY *is a consultant and executive of the Triwest Group, which develops programs for public mental health systems.*

7

Mental health services have generally ignored the parenting needs of women with serious mental illness. This chapter identifies the parenting risks and strengths that these women display, as well as the opportunities available to psychologists to play a key role in improving mother and child outcomes.

Mothers with Serious Mental Illness

Carol T. Mowbray, Daphna Oyserman, Deborah Bybee

We're related to each other in ways we never fully understand, maybe hardly understand at all. He was always the real reason for coming out of the hospital. To have let him grow up alone would have been *really* wrong. . . . I haven't been carrying him at all. He's been carrying *me*!

Pirsig (1974, p. 409)

In the first half of the twentieth century, individuals with serious mental illness often spent most of their lives confined in institutions. Deinstitutionalization and the wider availability of community-based treatments produced many ramifications for consumers, families, service providers, and society at large. Often noted are the burdens placed on families to care for ill relatives, increased homelessness as individuals with mental illness were no longer housed by the state, transinstitutionalization (discharging older adults with mental illness into nursing homes), and criminalization (numerous individuals with mental illness allegedly sent to jail for status offenses or minor crimes). The policy and practice changes developed to address or prevent these problems have included family education and support services, increased residential options (independent and dependent living) with housing supports provided, stricter laws and procedures governing Medicare reimbursements for skilled nursing home care, jail diversion programs, and education and training (supported employment and supported education)

This study was supported by a research grant from the National Institute of Mental Health, R01-54321, Mental Health Services Research Branch, to the University of Michigan, School of Social Work.

through psychosocial rehabilitation, and vocational rehabilitation programs, designed to move more individuals into self-sufficiency.

What is seldom recognized are the implications of deinstitutionalization for marriage, childbearing, and the parenting roles of individuals with serious mental illness. Indeed, although a substantial body of literature addresses the problems of children whose parents have a psychiatric disability, there are relatively few research data available, especially with diverse populations, on the number and characteristics of parents with mental illness, their strengths and deficits, and how these factors affect parenting quality. Nor is there much documentation or shared knowledge among mental health researchers or practitioners. When Daphna Oyserman and I undertook our first grant application to the National Institute of Mental Health, "Women with a Serious Mental Illness: Coping with Parenthood," we received mixed responses. Some colleagues reacted with disbelief that this was even a population for us to study: "Do female mental patients have children? Can they keep them?" On the other hand were responses like, "Why study mentally ill women with children? How is their situation different from that of any other low-income, urban sample of mothers?"

The gaps in our professional research and practice knowledge base concerning the interrelationships between parenting and mental illness are such that one might find a deeper understanding in humanities and literature, exemplified by the quotation from *Zen and the Art of Motorcycle Maintenance* at the beginning of this chapter. *Zen* is a narrative of a motorcycle adventure undertaken by the main character and his son. Although we are given hints throughout the story, we do not learn until the end of the book that this father has been seriously mentally ill and previously institutionalized; he has consciously suppressed these experiences. However, in the last chapter, the father realizes that his previous belief—that *he* was supporting his son, Chris—was wrong, and it is the other way around: that it is *his* role as a parent and *his* contacts with his son that have supported him in recovery from mental illness.

In this chapter, we seek to correct some of the deficiencies in the professional literature on parenting and mental illness concerning the demographics of parents with a mental illness, the risk factors and supports they experience, their parenting attitudes and behaviors, and what predicts parenting outcomes. The information presented comes from the available literature and our ongoing study of women with serious mental illness who are mothers. We put special emphasis on our own findings for several reasons, including the fact that we are proud of the quality and completeness of the data; we know the effort in time and resources required to assemble this database, and we are consequently motivated to see its findings used. Equally important, we believe that this is the largest U.S. longitudinal study undertaken of mothering among women with mental illness, recruited from the public sector, an especially important point, since it means that this sample has much diversity and differs substantially from many other studies, which have typically involved samples overrepresenting women who are married, white, or middle income (see, for example, Oyserman, Mowbray, Allen-Meares, and Firminger, 2000).

In the MOMS study (our nickname for the NIMH grant on Coping with Motherhood),[1] women were recruited from community mental health centers (CMHCs) and hospitals serving public patients in metropolitan Detroit. The following criteria were used for including women in the study: ages between eighteen and fifty-five, with a serious mental illness (duration greater than a year; diagnoses primarily of schizophrenia, major affective disorder, or bipolar disorder; and causing major dysfunction in one or more life areas), and having care responsibilities for at least one child between the ages of four and sixteen. Participants were 60 percent African American, 29 percent Caucasian, 8 percent Hispanic, and 3 percent other racial and ethnic groups. Except for an overrepresentation of Hispanics (which was purposeful, to allow separate examination of data from this subgroup), the demographics mirrored the composition of the population in treatment in the catchment area, according to statistics produced by the local community mental health board. The women in our study represented a wide range of educational levels, with 40 percent having some college or beyond, 25 percent a high school diploma or general equivalency diploma, and 35 percent less than a high school education. Participants' median age was 36.2 years. Out of 484 eligible women identified from CMHCs or inpatient units, 59 (12 percent) refused and 46 (10 percent) could not be contacted or scheduled, resulting in a baseline sample size of 379. These women were given a Diagnostic Interview Schedule (NIMH, 1980) by trained interviewers and also interviewed about their demographics, including living arrangements, clinical history, symptoms, and community functioning, as well as their parenting attitudes, behaviors, and beliefs.

Parenting and Mental Illness: Demographic Data

The research indicates that many persons with mental illness have children. Women with mental illness have normal fertility rates and bear an average or above-average number of children (Saugstad, 1989; Buckley, Buchanan, Schulz, and Tamminga, 1996); reports range from 1.9 to 2.4 children (1.9, Wang and Goldschmidt, 1994; 2.0, Caton, Cournos, Felix, and Wyatt, 1998; 2.1, Zemencuk, Rogosch, and Mowbray, 1995; 2.2, Nicholson, Sweeney, and Geller, 1998a; 2.4, Nicholson, Nason, Calabresi, and Yando, 1999). In the MOMS study, the 379 women in our sample were mothers of 1,082 children, or a median of three children per mother. Research indicates that the vast majority of persons with mental illness who are identified as parents are women (Nicholson, Nason, Calabresi, and Yando, 1999); women with mental illness are more likely to marry than men (National Institute of Mental Health, 1986) and are less likely to be childless (Saugstad, 1989). Ten to 15 percent of pregnant women develop a mental illness postpartum (Downey and Coyne, 1990; Oates, 1988).

Data are less clear concerning the extent to which women with mental illness who are mothers are carrying out parenting responsibilities. Reported estimates are that 9 percent of females receive intensive case management services, 10 percent of women are in mental health–supported housing (Blanch and Purcell, 1993), 25 percent are dually diagnosed clients (Schwab, Clark, and Drake, 1991), 32.5 percent are Assertive Community Treatment clients (Test, Burke, and Wallisch, 1990), and 46 percent of adult females are receiving routine case management (White, Nicholson, Fisher, and Geller, 1995). In the MOMS study, we calculated that about one-third of a possible 1,315 women, listed in the management information systems of the three largest agencies, had minor children as dependents (Mowbray and others, 2000b). Although these estimates of prevalence vary widely, even the lowest of these rates would indicate that parenting is a substantial issue that needs to be addressed for women with mental illness. It is also not clear the extent to which mothers with serious mental illness lose custody of their children, with reported lifetime rates ranging from 28 percent to 60 percent (Miller and Finnerty, 1996; Bazar, 1990; Coverdale and Aruffo, 1989; Test, Burke, and Wallisch, 1990). Analyses of some court decisions concerning termination of parental rights for women with serious mental illness suggest that these women may experience discrimination ("Termination of Parental Rights," 1985, 1986a, 1986b), and according to some state statutes, custody can be lost through diagnosis of mental illness per se, absent any allegations of abuse or neglect. In any case, custody concerns figure prominently for mothers with mental illness (Cook and Steigman, 2000).

Risk Factors and Lack of Support for Parenting

As is the case for many persons with psychiatric disabilities (Rogler, 1996), mothers with long-term mental illness are usually poor (Goodman and Johnson, 1986). In our MOMS study, more than two-thirds were living below the poverty line, 78 percent were currently unemployed (Mowbray and others, 2000a), 41 percent received federal welfare assistance (Aid to Families with Dependent Children/Temporary Assistance to Needy Families), and 48 percent were on Supplemental Security Income or Social Security Disability Income. Not surprisingly, 57 percent of these mothers were not satisfied with their financial situation. The income levels of these women were substantially lower than those of other adults living in the same census tracts (Mowbray and others, 2000b).

Mothers with mental illness are more often divorced or never married, raising their children as single parents (Cohn and others, 1986; Downey and Coyne, 1990; Mowbray, Oyserman, and Ross, 1995; Rogosch, Mowbray, and Bogat, 1992). In the MOMS study, only 40 percent of participants were currently married or living with a partner; the remainder were equally likely to be never married or previously married (Mowbray and others, 2000b). Even those women with a mental illness who are married often experience marital conflict (Cox, Puckering, Pound, and Mills, 1987; Downey and Coyne, 1990; Krener, Simmons, Hansen, and Treat, 1989) and are more likely to marry a spouse with a psychiatric disorder (Keitner and Miller, 1990; Lancaster, 1999; Rutter and Quinton, 1984). When depressed persons have psychiatrically disturbed spouses, their own symptoms are more severe, and marital disturbance is more likely (Puckering, 1989; Quinton, Rutter, and Liddle, 1984).

Social support for mothers with mental illness is problematic in a number of other ways. Support or assistance received from the fathers of their children is typically low (Mowbray, Oyserman, and Ross, 1995). Conflicts with extended family are reportedly common (Nicholson, Sweeney, and Geller, 1998b), as is social isolation (Cox, Puckering, Pound, and Mills, 1987; Downey and Coyne, 1990). In the MOMS study population, the average number of supporters in women's social networks was significantly lower than that of a less disabled mental health population but comparable to that of other disadvantaged women (Mowbray and others, 2000a). The stress of parenting under conditions of poverty, social isolation, and marital discord is known to decrease sensitive and responsive parenting behaviors (Miller-Loncar, Landry, Smith, and Swank, 1997) and increase risks for negative outcomes in children (Davies and Windle, 1997; Hops and others, 1987), likely causing further stress and symptomatology for mothers.

Women with a mental illness also tend to live in adverse physical environments. Pregnant women with severe mental illness were often undomiciled or homeless according to several research studies (Miller, 1990; Rudolph and others, 1990), and in qualitative research, these mothers have reported difficulty finding acceptable housing for themselves and their children (Sands, 1995). MOMS study participants reported mixed feelings about their neighbors and neighborhood safety, appearance, and cleanliness, rating their neighborhoods substantially lower than did a comparable national sample (Mowbray and others, 2000b).

Besides these stressors from living arrangements and relationships, mothers with serious mental illness are subject to stressful life histories and current living circumstances. Research on incidence rates of childhood abuse demonstrates a significantly higher occurrence among women with mental illness compared to the general adult female population (Siegel and others, 1987). Incidence of childhood sexual assault reported by female psychiatric patients ranges from 20 to 51 percent in inpatient settings and 22 to 54 percent in outpatient settings, compared to 6 to 15 percent for the general population (Bifulco, Brown, and Adler, 1991).

Mothers with mental illness also experience more negative recent life events (Webster-Stratton and Hammond, 1988). In the MOMS study, half or more of the respondents reported experiencing the following in the previous twelve months: a psychiatric crisis, major money crisis, or the death of a close friend or relative. Furthermore, more than one-third reported major separations from their children or a serious illness or injury to themselves, and one in seven reported being physically or sexually assaulted (Mowbray and others, 2000a). Participants in the MOMS study had significantly worse health status than a comparable sample of women who were aged eighteen to forty-five, of lower economic status, and living in a midwestern city (Mowbray and others, 2000a).

Treatment Availability

Accessible and appropriate mental health services should ameliorate the effects of these risk factors. Unfortunately, needed mental health services are often not available to adults with serious mental illness. Nationally, mental health service as a percentage of health care expenditures has recently been declining; historically, services to persons with serious mental illness have been inadequately funded and insufficiently available (Mechanic and McAlpine, 1999). The mental health services that are provided often decontextualize individuals with serious mental illness from their environments, seeing only "patients" and not people. So, for example, histories of current or past sexual abuse among women with serious mental illness are seldom explored by mental health professionals (Jacobson and Richardson, 1987). According to a New York statewide task force, mental health providers generally view service recipients as patients rather than as family members or parents (Blanch, Nicholson, and Purcell, 1994). It is thus not surprising that parenting and child care concerns are usually ignored by mental health providers who are working with adults with serious mental illness. That is, the extent to which women enrolled in ongoing mental health interventions typically receive treatment that addresses or even considers their needs as mothers or the needs of their children appears to be minimal. For example, 44 percent of psychiatric inpatient records at a private teaching hospital did not indicate whether the patient had children; when parenthood was documented, the whereabouts of children was recorded in only 20 percent of cases, and children were contacted in only 32 percent of cases (DeChillo, Matorin, and Hallahan, 1987). In a state psychiatric hospital study, only 19 percent of records of mothers mentioned the woman's children. Few state information systems even collect data about whether mentally ill patients have young children (Nicholson, Geller, Fisher, and Dion, 1993). And this situation is not confined to American psychiatry: in a Danish study, 40 percent of psychiatric inpatients had never received professional help related to their children, despite the fact that child psychiatrists who were reviewing records found "reason for concern" in regard to 77 percent of these children. Contrary to prevalent assumptions, 80 percent of these parents when interviewed said they would not be afraid to ask for help; only 10 percent mentioned fear of the authorities as a basis for their reluctance to seek assistance (Wang and Goldschmidt, 1996).

Not only are risks for mother and child often ignored by mental health professionals, but women with a serious mental illness may receive more services to help them cope with daily living tasks when they do not have children or child care responsibilities than when they do. Thus, it has recently been argued that in Great Britain, sheltered living environments (such as group homes) are provided only to women not caring for children; women with children must either make it on their own or lose custody of their child (Perkins, 1992). We were unable to find any published evaluation of an ongoing program in the United States that provides a sheltered living environment for mothers with mental illness and their children. Cook and Steigman (2000) have recently described supported housing and residential programming specifically designed for consumer parents. A number of specialized outpatient programs supporting mothers with serious mental illness have also been reported (Cohler and Musick, 1983; Cook and Steigman, 2000; Gonzales and others, 1991; Oates, 1988; Stott and others, 1984; Tableman, 1987; Waldo, Roath, Levine, and Freedman, 1987), although their numbers are limited. Unfortunately, available evaluations document high dropout rates in long-term programs, and studies using careful research designs have been unable to document improved outcomes resulting from such programs (Oyserman, Mowbray, and Zemencuk, 1994).

In the MOMS study, the vast majority of participants (96 percent) reported having used some type of mental health services during the past three months—typically outpatient or case management. Overall, mental health services were seen as "somewhat helpful" by participants. However, on a specific item concerning how much their mental health services helped with the problems of being a parent, women's responses were significantly lower, on average, than for the other eight scale items. Furthermore, when asked to whom they would turn for support and advice about being a mother, only about 20 percent of respondents listed a mental health provider (Mowbray and others, 2000a). Approximately half of the respondents provided an answer to an open-ended question about additional mental health services they needed. Responses mentioned by 25 percent or more included more control over therapy, availability of group therapy and self-help, child care and help with transportation, more financial resources, and skill training in parenting or household management. In another small, qualitative study, mothers with mental illness mentioned the need for assistance in financial and household management (Mowbray, Oyserman, and Ross, 1995). A Danish study of psychiatric inpatients found that about one-third expressed a need for additional assistance with their children, mainly involving accessing child psychotherapy, relationships with foster care families, assistance with improving parenting competence, and practical help at home. Many of these patients emphasized the importance of offering help at an early stage and of involving the whole family in better understanding the parent's mental illness (Wang and Goldschmidt, 1996).

At-Risk Parenting

According to our recent review (Oyserman, Mowbray, Allen-Meares, and Firminger, 2000), research studies have consistently found that with children aged preschool and older, mothers with a serious mental illness, in comparison to non–mentally ill mothers, are significantly less emotionally available, less reciprocal, less involved, less positive (Musick and others, 1984; Stott and others, 1984), less encouraging (Scherer and others, 1996), less affectionate and responsive (Goodman and Brumley, 1990), less able to differentiate their own needs from those of the child (Cohler and others, 1980), and more disorganized and inconsistent (Davenport, Zahn-Waxler, Adland, and Mayfield, 1984).

Maternal mental illness is clearly a risk factor for children. Children whose mothers have a long-term, serious mental illness are at increased risk of being placed in alternative settings such as foster care (Oyserman, Ben-ishty, and Ben Rabi, 1992), and in their lifetimes, from one-third to more than half of these children will themselves have a diagnosable disorder (Amminger and others, 1999; Jacobsen, Miller, and Kirkwood, 1997; Waters and Marchenko-Bouer, 1980). Early childhood and early to mid-adolescence appear to be the ages of heightened risk, according to Beardslee and Whee-lock (1994). These authors note the lack of attention to treatment or prevention services for children of depressed parents.

In the MOMS study, we asked mothers to complete a Child Behavior Checklist (Achenbach and Edelbrock, 1983) on a target child, typically one of school age. Age-adjusted comparisons showed that scores of all groups of children differed significantly from those of a normative sample. Furthermore, the overall behavioral problems of girls as well as the internalizing behavior problems of boys were comparable to those of clinical samples (Mowbray and others, 2000b).

Some of the association between the psychiatric problems of mothers and their children may reflect the heritability of major mental illnesses (estimated at 80 percent for bipolar disorder, 34 to 48 percent for depression, and 75 percent for schizophrenia; Rutter, Silberg, O'Connor, and Siminoff, 1999). However, according to other research, mental illness in offspring reflects significantly less adequate parenting skills and behaviors in these mothers compared to those of non–mentally ill mothers (Oyserman, Mowbray, Allen-Meares, and Firminger, 2000). Our own research suggests a limited relationship between mothers' diagnoses and parenting variables; contextual factors and mothers' current symptomatology and functioning play a much larger role.

Many existing studies of the parenting of women with serious mental illness display serious gaps. Consistently this research has employed a deficit perspective, examining only mothers' problems, not their strengths. Data are collected from mental health providers, clinical records, behavioral observations, or quantified self-report questionnaires, with only limited options for describing positive parenting. Positive parenting is more likely to emerge from qualitative assessments of how women feel about children and the mothering role, which allow women's answers and perspectives to emerge rather than being fit into investigator-predetermined, deficit, and problem-oriented categories. Finally, the research has been extremely limited in its efforts to examine systematically the effects of environmental factors like economic levels, social support, or culture on parenting outcomes. This is a severe limitation, since mental illness covaries significantly with numerous socioeconomic factors that also predict problematic parenting, such as poverty level, stressful life events, single parenthood, isolation, and lack of support (Oyserman, Mowbray, Allen-Meares, and Firminger, 2000).

Parenting: The Mothers' Perspective

In the MOMS project, we attempted to correct for some of the deficiencies in previous studies. Thus, we included a number of different ways to ask women about their orientation to parenting. We asked mothers in the study about the importance of the parenting role in comparison to other adult roles. We found that their ratings of the parenting role item averaged at the upper end of the scale—the highest mean and the lowest variance of all eleven family, personal, and social or work roles rated, indicating its primacy in women's self-perceptions. Women also reported high parenting satisfaction (averaging nearly 4, on a 5-point scale); parenting stress (Parenting Stress Index, Abidin, 1990) was reported at midrange on average (Mowbray and others, 2000b).

To get additional information on the participants' perspectives, each woman was asked a series of six open-ended questions concerning the advantages and disadvantages of motherhood, something that made her feel really good or really bad about being a mother, changes in her life brought on by motherhood, and what about being a mother was most important to her. These answers were coded into categories that encompassed six domains: personal benefits and personally rewarding aspects of motherhood (for example, having children means there is someone to help you and keep you company); personal stress due to parenting (for example, being a mother means being worried about what may happen to the child); motherhood as providing support and developmental context for the child (for example, being a mother means cleaning and cooking for a child and giving him or her love); the child as a burden (for example, being a mother means suffering through children's tantrums and bad behavior); motherhood as a valued social role (for example, being a mother means sharing holidays and other times with family and friends and feeling fulfilled as a woman); and mental illness as an aspect of motherhood (for example, being a mother means being careful with medication and staying in treatment because of children).

For nearly all participants, motherhood involved a focus on the child, and children were primarily perceived as a resource—a source of emotional support and positive self-feelings. Motherhood and being a parent are clearly central and important roles to many of the mothers in the study. In the words of one mother, "Motherhood has fulfilled my life. I don't know what I'd do without my kids. That's the God's honest truth. I don't know what I'd do without my kids." Over 90 percent of mothers mentioned provision of care and support to their children and the personal benefits of motherhood, and almost three-fourths of women saw motherhood as an important social role. In addition, though, about half described motherhood in terms of the burden of child rearing, and about 30 percent of mothers mentioned dealing with their mental illness. Motherhood was a source of personal stress for most.

Thus, to these women with mental illness, motherhood is simultaneously critical to personal happiness and also a source of everyday psychological distress; it means both the provision and the receipt of love and support and is a social role that carries status in society. On a day-to-day basis, motherhood means shared experiences and provides a reason to stop personally destructive behavior and to deal with one's mental illness. But motherhood is also perceived as a constraint, a role that takes away personal freedom—one that exacerbates feelings of inadequacy and lack of control. Finally, for many mothers, motherhood carries with it straining economically and forces them to deal with stressful child-rearing and discipline issues.

These results parallel those from other recent research, identifying the positive and motivating effects of parenting for individuals with psychiatric disabilities. In these smaller, qualitative studies, mothers with serious mental illness have identified motherhood as a central force for keeping them involved in treatment, a key outlet for expression of feelings of care and concern, and a valued, normative social role (Mowbray, Oyserman, and Ross, 1995; Nicholson, Sweeney, and Geller, 1998a; Perkins, 1992; Sands, 1995).

Predictors of Parenting Attitudes and Behaviors

Research is quite consistent concerning the problematic outcomes for children of mothers with mental illness and the fact that these mothers are significantly different compared to non–mentally ill mothers on their positive parenting attitudes and behaviors. Many factors in the mothers' clinical histories have been proposed to account for these differences. Studies have, in fact, found significant relationships between parenting measures and diagnosis (for example, Downey and Coyne, 1990; Hammen, 1997), current severity of disorder (Radke-Yarrow, Nottelmann, Belmont, and Welsh, 1993; Frankel and Harmon, 1996), and chronicity (Gross, 1983; Rogosch, Mowbray, and Bogat, 1992). However, so far nothing in the published literature has identified the independent effects of each of these clinical history variables (diagnosis, symptom severity, chronicity) or their effects independent of co-occurring conditions.

Since clinical characteristics of mothers with serious mental illness are so heterogeneous and vary by demographic variables such as poverty status, research on parenting outcomes should use multivariate techniques with covariate control variables to address this complexity. A few studies have done this. Gordon and others (1989), through a series of hierarchical regression analyses, established that chronic stress was a significant and independent predictor of maternal communication quality above and beyond the contribution of current symptoms. Hamilton, Jones, and Hammen (1993) reported that high levels of chronic stress, lower rates of positive life events, and single parenthood were significant predictors of affective style for mothers with mental illness. Once these variables were taken into account, maternal diagnostic status was not a significant predictor. Finally, a longitudinal study of mothers from an inner London borough found little evidence of maternal depression predicting child behavior problems after differences in socioenvironmental stressors (such as overcrowding) were taken into account (Ghodsian, Zajicek, and Wolkind, 1984).

In our own research, we have found that positive parenting attitudes and viewing the child as a burden (variables obtained through scaling of responses from the meaning of motherhood questions) were both significant predictors of scores on Parental Nurturance (subscale of the Block Child Rearing Practices Scale; Rickel and Biasatti, 1982) and the Parenting Stress Index (Abidin, 1990). These dimensions of the meaning of motherhood are in turn predicted by variables such as the extent of daily hassles, community functioning, having a substance abuse history, and number of people available for social support (Oyserman, Bybee, Mowbray, and Kahng, 2000). The results suggest that women's parenting practices can be affected by their attitudes toward their children and seeing themselves as efficacious parents. Parenting practices are also affected by the context in which women live—the extent of hassles and economic stressors versus available social support. These are all variables that may be affected by treatment and prevention interventions, many of which have been developed, evaluated, and disseminated by psychologists.

Roles for Psychologists in Improving Services to Mothers with Serious Mental Illness

In other reports (Mowbray, Oyserman, Lutz, and Purnell, 1997; Oyserman, Mowbray, Allen-Meares, and Firminger, 2000), we have identified a number of service implications based on our own results and those reported in the literature. Intervention strategies noted include education and building awareness in clinicians, parenting assessments, and special programs developed for psychiatric consumers who are mothers. These recommended service activities follow.

• Educating clinicians to the likelihood that women with a serious mental illness have or will have children, and that parenthood needs to be an important component of treatment planning and case management services from their initiation. Psychologists have already demonstrated with diverse subgroups of non–mentally ill parents that children play an important role in adult social status and meaningfulness of women's lives. Psychologists need to be involved in services to persons with psychiatric disabilities and share these same conclusions with providers. Joanne Nicholson, a psychologist in the Department of Psychiatry at University of Massachusetts Medical School, is forging new awareness of parenting issues for adults with serious mental illness through her Parenting Options Project. In collaboration with the Massachusetts Department of Mental Health and funded through the National Institute on Disability and Rehabilitation Research, this project is developing resources for these parents, conducting workshops for service providers, and supporting the development of specialized services for parents statewide and at select clubhouse locations.

• Offering relevant periodic assessments of children in response to mothers' concerns and in order to determine changing needs for parenting resources and supports. The particular focus of each assessment will be individually based but could include, for example, testing and observation of children's attachment, social skills, and early signs and symptoms of mental and emotional disorders. For the mothers, as part of annual treatment planning, assessments of parenting should be offered, to include parenting stress, skills, and knowledge; attitudes and feelings toward nurturing and discipline of children; and parenting style. Assessments should also include mothers' past and current histories of experiencing interpersonal violence; separations from their children and their parents; available social support and parenting role models; living arrangements; negative life events; and chronic stressors—factors that can affect positive parenting and have often been identified as problematic for women with serious mental illness. The mother's situation regarding these variables is likely to affect her ability to parent significantly and the type of interventions that are warranted.

Psychologists are well trained in assessments of children and adults. They need to be aware of factors that are specifically relevant to women with mental illnesses (such as current or past histories of physical and sexual assault) and ensure that their skills also encompass assessment of these contextual and external circumstances. Nicholson, through the Parenting Options Project, has developed an assessment of parenting strengths and needs specifically designed with and for parents with severe mental illness (Cook and Steigman, 2000).

• Offering education and skill training for all female consumers who are parents. Many research reports, from clinician judgments and based on stated preferences of consumers, are converging in the need for mothers with mental illness to increase their skills in household and money management, because finances often put them below the poverty level and economic problems can create extreme financial stress, especially when they have to deny children's requests. Many mothers with mental illness have also mentioned their difficulties in determining whether, how, and when to provide information about their mental illness to their children and other family members. Some research suggests that children who understand and accept the parent's mental illness as separate from their own functioning have fewer problems (Beardslee and Podorefsky, 1988). Thus, psychiatric rehabilitation programs should consistently incorporate this information in service delivery.

Psychologists have particular skills and experience in developing interventions on coping and problem solving, particularly for disadvantaged populations. Thus, their backgrounds would enable them to make contributions in this development area, as well as to train staff to implement such educational interventions. To be most effective, the development of parenting interventions must meaningfully involve consumers who are parents: "Nothing about us without us."

• Ensuring availability of specialized individualized or group treatment for mothers and their families. Some women will need this more intensive form of service from their mental health agencies. Williams (1998) suggests providing joint parent-child therapy or psychoeducation for the entire family, to address the fact that children often feel ignorant about a parent's mental illness and mothers express difficulty in knowing how to discuss their mental illness with their children. Parent training has been frequently mentioned by mothers with mental illness in research and needs assessment studies. Parent support groups have been found to have significantly positive effects on the parenting of low-income women and other women with disadvantages. However, so that mothers can feel comfortable getting the help they need and discussing how to deal with their symptoms, such groups need to be exclusively for mothers with mental illness and within an agency or self-help setting. The use of generic parenting programs is not likely to be helpful due to the stigma still associated with mental illness.

Psychologists have conceptualized, developed, and researched a number of interventions for disadvantaged parents and their children. Taylor and Biglan (1998) reviewed published evidence on parenting interventions and concluded that behavioral family training is effective in improving child rearing in distressed families. Furthermore, for parents with additional issues, such as depression, training on child management strategies can be effectively enhanced by adding other components, such as training in personal and marital adjustment and self-control. Webster-Stratton has developed a comprehensive videotape-based parenting training that has proven effective in clinical treatment programs for families with conduct-disordered children and in community programs for at-risk families (Brestan and Eyberg, 1998; Taylor, Schmidt, Pepler, and Hodgins, 1998; Webster-Stratton and Herbert, 1994; Webster-Stratton and Hancock, 1998; Webster-Stratton and Taylor, 1998). The program's goals are strengthening parent competence, increasing positive family support networks and school involvement, promoting child social competence, and decreasing child conduct problems. These goals are highly congruent with the needs expressed by mothers with serious mental illness and relevant to the problems identified by research on these families.

Taylor and Biglan (1998) noted that therapists using these approaches need to have a high level of clinical skill in order to make the process of therapy collaborative. Doctorate-level psychology training should be optimal for effectively delivering these services. However, psychologists will need to increase their involvement with mothers with mental illness in order to understand their perspective, so that these interventions can be appropriately modified for these mothers.

• Carrying out more high-quality and comprehensive research on mothers with serious mental illness, to identify specific capabilities and risk factors in mothers' parenting practices that relate directly to child outcomes, as well as the direct and mediating roles on parenting of the social and economic contexts in which these women live. More research is also needed on the effectiveness of various service alternatives in place or being developed to meet the needs of these mothers best. Other priorities for research include the effects of parental mental illness on children in different developmental stages (adolescence is particularly understudied), as well as the interaction between parenting characteristics and individual child characteristics and temperament.

Psychologists have played major roles in studying the parenting of other populations and in evaluating parenting interventions. Once they become more involved in practice and research with individuals who are mentally ill, they will find that existing skills readily apply. The conceptualizations of motherhood articulated by the women with serious mental illness in our study have much in common with the perspectives of other low-income and disadvantaged mothers.

Conclusion

Mothers with mental illness confront many challenges in living and in raising their children. Children of these mothers are at high risk for diagnosed mental illness, substance abuse, and other problems in coping and behavior. Nevertheless, the role of parent is an important one for most women with mental illness and offers significant rehabilitation potential and motivation for recovery. Despite the challenges and opportunities, these mothers and their children have been largely ignored by mental health service systems. This situation is extremely unfortunate, since effective models of service do exist that could be extremely helpful to families where parents have mental illness. Psychologists could play key roles in delivering such services. However, before this can happen, an awareness of the needs and intervention possibilities for persons with psychiatric disabilities needs to be communicated in psychology preservice training and professional training provided through continuing-education seminars offered by the American Psychological Association, its state psychological associations, and individual colleges and universities. Without this push, psychologists will probably continue to avoid this client group, to the disadvantage of all. As self-help approaches and managed care oversight continue to decrease the marketplace for psychological services to less distressed populations, psychology needs to step up to the challenge of working with serious mental illness—for the benefit of the profession, adult consumers, and future generations of their children.

References

Abidin, R. *Parental Stress Index Test Manual*. (3rd ed.) Charlottesville, Va.: Pediatric Psychological Press, 1990.

Achenbach, T. M., and Edelbrock, C. *Manual for the Child Behavior Checklist and Revised Child Behavior Profile*. Burlington: University of Vermont, Department of Psychiatry, 1983.

Amminger, G., and others. "Relationship Between Childhood Behavioral Disturbance and Later Schizophrenia in the New York High-Risk Project." *American Journal of Psychiatry*, 1999, *156*(4), 525–530.

Bazar, J. "Mentally Ill Moms Aided in Keeping Their Children." *Monitor*, Dec. 1990, p. 32.

Beardslee, W., and Podorefsky, D. "Resilient Adolescents Whose Parents Have Serious Affective and Other Psychiatric Disorders: Importance of Self-Understanding and Relationships." *American Journal of Psychiatry*, 1988, *145*(1), 63–69.

Beardslee, W., and Wheelock, I. "Children of Parents with Affective Disorders." In W. Reynolds and H. Johnston (eds.), *Handbook of Depression in Children and Adolescents*. New York: Plenum Press, 1994.

Bifulco, A., Brown, G. W., and Adler, Z. "Early Sexual Abuse and Clinical Depression in Adult Life." *British Journal of Psychiatry*, 1991, *159*, 115–122.

Blanch, A., Nicholson, J., and Purcell, J. "Parents with Severe Mental Illness and Their Children: The Need for Human Services Integration." *Journal of Mental Health Administration*, 1994, *21*(4), 388–396.

Blanch, A., and Purcell, J. "Final Report: Task Force on Mentally Ill Parents With Young Children." Albany: New York State Office of Mental Health; New York State Department of Social Services, March 29, 1993.

Brestan, E. V., and Eyberg, S. M. "Effective Psychosocial Treatments of Conduct-Disordered Children and Adolescents: 29 Years, 82 Studies, and 5,272 Kids." *Journal of Consulting and Clinical Psychology*, 1998, *66*(1), 180–190.

Buckley, P., Buchanan, R., Schulz, S., and Tamminga, C. "Catching Up on Schizophrenia: The Fifth International Congress on Schizophrenia Research." *Archives of General Psychiatry*, 1996, *53*, 456–462.

Caton, C.L.M., Cournos, F., Felix, A., and Wyatt, R. J. "Childhood Experiences and Current Adjustment of Offspring of Indigent Patients with Schizophrenia." *Psychiatric Services*, 1998, *49*(1), 86–90.

Cohler, B. J., and others. "Childcare Attitudes and Development of Young Children of Mentally Ill and Well Mothers." *Psychological Reports*, 1980, *46*(1), 31–46.

Cohler, B. J., and Musick, J. S. "Psychopathology of Parenthood: Implications for Mental Health of Children." *Infant Mental Health Journal*, 1983, *4*(3), 140–163.

Cohn, J. F., and others. "Face to Face Interactions of Depressed Mothers and Their Infants." *New Directions for Child Development, 34*, 1986, 31–45.

Cook, J., and Steigman, P. "Experiences of Parents with Mental Illnesses and Their Service Needs." *Journal of NAMI California,* 2000, *11*(2), 21–23.

Coverdale, J. H., and Aruffo, J. A. "Family Planning Needs of Female Chronic Psychiatric Outpatients." *American Journal of Psychiatry,* 1989, *146*(11), 1489–1491.

Cox, A. D., Puckering, C., Pound, A., and Mills, M. "The Impact of Maternal Depression in Young Children." *Journal of Child Psychology and Psychiatry and Allied Disciplines,* 1987, *28*(6), 917–928.

Davenport, Y. B., Zahn-Waxler, C., Adland, M. L., and Mayfield, A. "Early Child Rearing Practices in Families with a Manic-Depressive Parent." *American Journal of Psychiatry,* 1984, *141*(2), 230–235.

Davies, P., and Windle, M. "Gender-Specific Pathways Between Maternal Depressive Symptoms, Family Discord, and Adolescent Adjustment." *Developmental Psychology,* 1997, *33*(4), 657–668.

DeChillo, N., Matorin, S., and Hallahan, C. "Children of Psychiatric Patients: Rarely Seen or Heard." *Health and Social Work,* 1987, *12*(4), 296–302.

Downey, G., and Coyne, J. C. "Children of Depressed Parents—an Integrative Review." *Psychological Bulletin,* 1990, *108*(1), 50–76.

Frankel, K., and Harmon, R. "Depressed Mothers: They Don't Always Look as Bad as They Feel." *Journal of the American Academy of Child and Adolescent Psychiatry,* 1996, *35*(3), 289–298.

Ghodsian, M., Zajicek, E., and Wolkind, S. "A Longitudinal-Study of Maternal Depression and Child-Behavior Problems." *Journal of Child Psychology and Psychiatry and Allied Disciplines,* 1984, *25*(1), 91–109.

Gonzales, L., and others. "Community Mental Health." In M. Hersen, A. Kazdin, and A. S. Bellack (eds.), *The Clinical Psychology Handbook.* New York: Pergamon Press, 1991.

Goodman, S. H., and Brumley, H. E. "Schizophrenic and Depressed Mothers—Relational Deficits in Parenting." *Developmental Psychology,* 1990, *26*(1), 31–39.

Goodman, S. H., and Johnson, M. S. "Life Problems, Social Supports, and Psychological Functioning of Emotionally-Disturbed and Well Low-Income Women." *Journal of Community Psychology,* 1986, *14*(2), 150–158.

Gordon, D., and others. "Observations of Interactions of Depressed Women with Their Children." *American Journal of Psychiatry,* 1989, *146*(1), 50–55.

Gross, D. "How Some Dyads 'Fail': A Qualitative Analysis with Implications for Nursing Practice." *Infant Mental Health Journal,* 1983, *4,* 272–286.

Hamilton, E. B., Jones, M., and Hammen, C. "Maternal Interaction Style in Affective Disordered, Physically Ill, and Normal Women." *Family Process,* 1993, *32*(3), 329–340.

Hammen, C. "Children of Depressed Parents: The Stress Context." In S. Wolchik (ed.), *Handbook of Children's Coping: Linking Theory and Intervention.* New York: Plenum Press, 1997.

Hops, H., and others. "Home Observations of Family Interactions of Depressed Women." *Journal of Consulting and Clinical Psychology,* 1987, *55,* 341–346.

Jacobsen, T., Miller, L. J., and Kirkwood, K. P. "Assessing Parenting Competency in Individuals with Severe Mental Illness: A Comprehensive Service." *Journal of Mental Health Administration,* 1997, *24*(2), 189–199.

Jacobson, A., and Richardson, B. "Assault Experiences of 100 Psychiatric Inpatients: Evidence of the Need for Routine Inquiry." *American Journal of Psychiatry,* 1987, *144*(7), 908–913.

Keitner, G. I., and Miller, I. W. "Family Functioning and Major Depression—an Overview." *American Journal of Psychiatry,* 1990, *147*(9), 1128–1137.

Krener, P., Simmons, M. K., Hansen, R. L., and Treat, J. N. "Effect of Pregnancy on Psychosis—Life Circumstances and Psychiatric-Symptoms." *International Journal of Psychiatry in Medicine,* 1989, *19*(1), 65–84.

Lancaster, S. "Being There: How Parental Mental Illness Can Affect Children." In V. Cowling (ed.), *Children of Parents with Mental Illness.* Melbourne: Australian Council for Educational Research, 1999.

Mechanic, D., and McAlpine, D. "Mission Unfulfilled: Potholes on the Road to Mental Health Parity." *Health Affairs,* 1999, *18*(95), 7–21.

Miller, L. J. "Psychotic Denial of Pregnancy—Phenomenology and Clinical Management." *Hospital and Community Psychiatry,* 1990, *419*(11), 1233–1237.

Miller, L. J., and Finnerty, M. "Sexuality, Pregnancy, and Child-Rearing Among Women with Schizophrenia-Spectrum Disorders." *Psychiatric Services,* 1996, *47*(95), 502–506.

Miller-Loncar, C. L., Landry, S. H., Smith, K. E., and Swank, P. R. "The Role of Child-Centered Perspectives in a Model of Parenting." *Journal of Experimental Child Psychology,* 1997, *66*(93), 341–361.

Mowbray, C. T., Oyserman, D., Lutz, C., and Purnell, R. "Women: The Ignored Majority." In L. Sponial, C. Gagne, and M. Koehler (Eds.), *Psychological and Social Aspects of Psychiatric Disability.* Boston: Center for Psychiatric Rehabilitation, 1997, 171–193.

Mowbray, C. T., Oyserman, D., and Ross, S. "Parenting and the Significance of Children for Women with a Serious Mental Illness." *Journal of Mental Health Administration,* 1995, *22*(2), 189–200.

Mowbray, C. T., and others. "Mothers with a Mental Illness: Stressors and Resources for Parenting and Living." *Families and Society,* 2000a, *81*(2), 118–129.

Mowbray, C. T., and others. "Life Circumstances of Mothers with Serious Mental Illness." Unpublished manuscript, 2000b.

Musick, J., and others. "The Capacity for 'Enabling' in Mentally Ill Mothers." *Zero to Three,* 1984, *4,* 1–6.

National Institute of Mental Health. *Diagnostic Interview Schedule DIS.* Rockville, Md.: National Institute of Mental Health, 1980.

National Institute of Mental Health. *Client/Patient Sample Survey of Inpatient, Outpatient, and Partial Care Programs.* Rockville, Md.: National Institute of Mental Health, 1986.

Nicholson, J., Geller, J. L., Fisher, W. H., and Dion, G. L. "State Policies and Programs That Address the Needs of Mentally Ill Mothers in the Public Sector." *Hospital and Community Psychiatry,* 1993, *44*(5), 484–489.

Nicholson, J., Nason, M. W., Calabresi, A. O., and Yando, R. "Fathers with Severe Mental Illness: Characteristics and Comparisons." *American Journal of Orthopsychiatry,* 1999, *69*(1), 134–141.

Nicholson, J., Sweeney, E. M., and Geller, J. L. "Mothers with Mental Illness: I. The Competing Demands of Parenting and Living with Mental Illness." *Psychiatric Services,* 1998a, *49*(5), 635–642.

Nicholson, J., Sweeney, E. M., and Geller, J. L. "Mothers with Mental Illness: II. Family Relationships and the Context of Parenting." *Psychiatric Services,* 1998b, *49*(5), 643–649.

Oates, M. "The Development of an Integrated Community-Orientated Service for Severe Postnatal Mental Illness." *Motherhood and Mental Illness,* 1988, *2,* 133–158.

Oyserman, D., Benbishty, R., and Ben Rabi, D. "Characteristics of Children and Their Families at Entry into Foster Care." *Psychiatry and Human Development,* 1992, *22,* 199–211.

Oyserman, D., Bybee, D., Mowbray, C. T., and Kahng, S. "Maternal Mental Illness and Parenting Self-Construals: Behavioral Correlates and Possible Antecedents of Parenting Efficacy." Unpublished manuscript, University of Michigan, 2000.

Oyserman, D., Mowbray, C. T., Allen-Meares, P., and Firminger, K. "Parenting Among Mothers with a Serious Mental Illness." *American Journal of Orthopsychiatry,* 2000, *70*(3), 296–315.

Oyserman, D., Mowbray, C. T., and Zemencuk, J. K. "Resources and Supports for Mothers with Severe Mental Illness." *Health and Social Work,* 1994, *19*(2), 132–142.

Perkins, R. "Catherine Is Having a Baby." *Feminism and Psychology,* 1992, *2*(1), 110–112.

Pirsig, R. *Zen and the Art of Motorcycle Maintenance.* New York: William Morrow & Co., 1974.

Puckering, C. "Annotation: Maternal Depression." *Journal of Child Psychology and Psychiatry and Allied Disciplines,* 1989, *30*(6), 807–817.

Quinton, D., Rutter, M., and Liddle, C. "Institutional Rearing, Parenting Difficulties and Marital Support." *Psychological Medicine,* 1984, *14,* 107–124.

Radke-Yarrow, M., Nottelmann, E., Belmont, B., and Welsh, J. D. "Affective Interactions of Depressed and Nondepressed Mothers and Their Children." *Journal of Abnormal Child Psychology,* 1993, *21,* 683–695.

Rickel, A., and Biasatti, L. "Modifications of the Block Child Rearing Practices." *Journal of Clinical Psychology,* 1982, *38,* 129–134.

Rogler, L. "Increasing Socioeconomic Inequalities and the Mental Health of the Poor." *Journal of Nervous and Mental Disease,* 1996, *184*(12), 719–722.

Rogosch, F. A., Mowbray, C. T., and Bogat, G. A. "Determinants of Parenting Attitudes in Mothers with Severe Psychopathology." *Development and Psychopathology,* 1992, *4,* 469–487.

Rudolph, B., and others. "Hospitalized Pregnant Psychotic Women—Characteristics and Treatment Issues." *Hospital and Community Psychiatry,* 1990, *41*(2), 159–163.

Rutter, M., and Quinton, D. "Parental Psychiatric Disorder: Effects on Children." *Psychological Medicine,* 1984, *14*(4), 853–880.

Rutter, M., Silberg, J., O'Connor, T., and Siminoff, E. "Genetics and Child Psychiatry: II. Empirical Research Findings." *Journal of Child Psychology and Psychiatry and Allied Disciplines,* 1999, *40*(1), 19–55.

Sands, R. G. "The Parenting Experience of Low-Income Single Women with Serious Mental Disorders." *Families in Society: The Journal of Contemporary Human Services,* 1995, *76*(2), 86–96.

Saugstad, L. F. "Social Class, Marriage, and Fertility in Schizophrenia." *Schizophrenia Bulletin,* 1989, *15*(1), 9–43.

Scherer, D., and others. "Relation Between Children's Perception of Maternal Mental Illness and Children's Psychological Adjustment." *Journal of Clinical Child Psychology,* 1996, *25,* 156–169.

Schwab, B., Clark, R. E., and Drake, R. E. "An Ethnographic Note on Clients as Parents." *Psychosocial Rehabilitation Journal,* 1991, *15*(2), 95–99.

Siegel, J. M., and others. "The Prevalence of Childhood Sexual Assault: The Los Angeles Epidemiologic Catchment Area Project." *American Journal of Epidemiology,* 1987, *126*(6), 1141–1153.

Stott, F. M., and others. "Intervention for the Severely Disturbed Mother." In J. Musick and B. Cohler (eds.), *Intervention Among Psychiatrically Impaired Parents and Their Young Children.* San Francisco: Jossey-Bass, 1984.

Tableman, B. "Stress Management Training: An Approach to the Prevention of Depression in Low-Income Populations." In R. Munoz (ed.), *Depression Prevention: Research Directions.* Washington, D.C.: Hemisphere Publishing Corp., 1987.

Taylor, T. K., and Biglan, A. "Behavioral Family Interventions for Improving Child-Rearing: A Review of the Literature for Clinicians and Policy Makers." *Clinical Child and Family Psychology Review,* 1998, *1*(1), 41–60.

Taylor, T. K., Schmidt, F., Pepler, D., and Hodgins, C. "A Comparison of Eclectic Treatment with Webster-Stratton's Parents and Children Series in a Children's Mental Health Center: A Randomized Controlled Trial." *Behavior Therapy,* 1998, *29,* 221–240.

"Termination of Parental Rights." *Mental and Physical Disability Law Reporter,* 1985, *9*(3), 187–189.

"Termination of Parental Rights-Mental Illness." *Mental and Physical Disability Law Reporter,* 1986a, *10*(2), 104–106.

Termination of Parental Rights-Mental Illness. *Mental and Physical Disability Law Reporter,* 1986b, *10*(3), 182–183.

Test, M. A., Burke, S. S., and Wallisch, L. S. "Gender Differences of Young Adults with Schizophrenic Disorders in Community Care." *Schizophrenia Bulletin,* 1990, *16*(2), 331–344.

Waldo, M. C., Roath, M., Levine, W., and Freedman, R. "A Model Program to Teach Parenting Skills to Schizophrenic Mothers." *Hospital and Community Psychiatry,* 1987, *38*(10), 1110–1112.

Wang, A., and Goldschmidt, V. "Interviews of Psychiatric Patients About Their Family Situation and Young Children." *Acta Psychiatrica Scandinavia,* 1994, *90,* 459–465.

Wang, A., and Goldschmidt, V. "Interviews with Psychiatric Inpatients About Professional Intervention with Regard to Their Children." *Acta Psychiatrica Scandinavica,* 1996, *93*(1), 57–61.

Waters, B.G.H., and Marchenko-Bouer, I. "Psychiatric Illness in the Adult Offspring of Bipolar Manic-Depressives." *Journal of Affective Disorders,* 1980, *2,* 119–126.

Webster-Stratton, C., and Hammond, M. "Maternal Depression and Its Relationship to Life Stress, Perceptions of Child Behavior Problems, Parenting Behaviors and Child Conduct Problems." *Journal of Abnormal Child Psychology,* 1988, *16,* 299–315.

Webster-Stratton, C., and Hancock, L. "Training for Parents of Young Children with Conduct Problems: Content, Methods, and Therapeutic Processes." In J. M. Briesmeister and C. E. Schaefer (eds.), *Handbook of Parent Training: Parents as Co-Therapists for Children's Behavior Problem.* New York: Wiley, 1998.

Webster-Stratton, C., and Herbert, M. 1994, *Troubled Families, Problem Children. Working With Parents: A Collaborative Process.* New York: Wiley.

Webster-Stratton, C., and Taylor, T. K. "Adopting and Implementing Empirically Supported Interventions: A Recipe for Success." In A. Buchanan and B. L. Hudson (eds.), *Parenting, Schooling and Children's Behaviour: Interdisciplinary Approaches.* Brookfield, Vt.: Ashgate Publishing, 1998.

White, C. L., Nicholson, J., Fisher, W. H., and Geller, J. L. "Mothers with Severe Mental Illness Caring for Children." *Journal of Nervous and Mental Disease,* 1995, *183*(6), 398–403.

Williams, A. S. "A Group for the Adult Daughters of Mentally Ill Mothers: Looking Backwards and Forwards." *British Journal of Medical Psychology,* 1998, *71,* 73–83.

Zemencuk, J., Rogosch, F. A., and Mowbray, C. T. "The Seriously Mentally Ill Woman in the Role of Parent Characteristics, Parenting Sensitivity, and Needs." *Psychosocial Rehabilitation Journal,* 1995, *18*(3), 77–92.

CAROL T. MOWBRAY is professor and associate dean for research at the University of Michigan School of Social Work. She is also the principal investigator on the NIMH-funded research project, "Seriously Mentally Ill Mothers Coping with Parenthood."

DAPHNA OYSERMAN is associate professor at the School of Social Work and Primary Research Scientist in the Institute for Social Research, University of Michigan. She is principal investigator on a NIMH-funded study "Pathways," researching the risk and resiliency factors of adolescent children of mothers with mental illness.

DEBORAH BYBEE is an associate professor in the Psychology Department at Michigan State University and has a private consulting practice in Williamston, Michigan.

8

The expertise gleaned from being a patient in a psychiatric hospital is used to train hospital staff in what is helpful to patients and what hurts. The trainers are consumers/survivors/ex-patients in different stages of recovery.

Consumers/Survivors/Ex-Patients as Change Facilitators

Ronald Bassman

After twenty-two years of living within the acceptable range of normality, my passage into schizophrenia was bewildering to my family. Psychiatrists looking back at my childhood history could perform a psychological autopsy and find warning signs of future mental illness, but those predictions could be made only after the label was already in place. My introduction to madness followed the norm for my diagnosis; I was twenty-two when I was first hospitalized, right in line with the median age for the onset of the first psychotic episode of schizophrenia. I was hospitalized twice for a total thirteen-month inpatient treatment: six months in a private hospital and, later, seven months in a public hospital.

When I was admitted to the hospital I was exhausted, fearful, suspicious, at times paranoid, and emotionally quite labile. Initially I was able to set aside those problems to pursue my most important goal: discharge. Actually right then, with that strong motivation, I was much clearer than the several days preceding my entrance into the hospital. I had pulled myself together for one last-stand battle to prove my sanity. But without help I could not sustain my effort at rationality. Society's soldiers, the guardians and keepers of chronic normalcy, would not allow me to move in and out of reality at my own discretion. The hospital workers spoke with one voice: "You will return the way we tell you or not at all."

The first weekend passed without my getting the opportunity to see a psychiatrist. All my yelling about being a voluntary patient and demanding to sign myself out was to no avail. Monday came and went without me. I got word that a psychiatrist was on the ward, but I was not given the chance to speak with him. He conferred with the nursing staff at their office, and they went over patient files. He saw no patients that day; he was too busy spending his half-hours on each ward making notes in patients' charts and approving medication orders. I requested an interview. I pleaded for an interview. I demanded an interview. I banged on the office door. The results: seclusion and more Thorazine. Monday drifted away.

I think it was a couple of days later that I again heard that the doctor was on the ward. There was also talk that he was seeing some patients. It was just medication review and questions for a few selected patients. When I saw that the door to his office was open, I stood there trying to make contact. I caught his attention and asked him if he would talk with me. The aides began to usher me away, but he stopped them and asked who I was. Then he flashed a magnanimous smile and said, "You'll have the opportunity to talk with me the next time I'm on the ward." I asked when that would be. "We'll see . . . maybe Friday." My stomach sank—more days and a maybe.

Slipping more and sliding down as if the floor was greased, I had no place to secure a grip. My ability to stay focused on my goal, discharge, had allowed me to mobilize some degree of clarity, but it was no longer working. Confusion grew daily, fed by my anger and exacerbated by the drugs. I was alone, isolated, and unable to communicate or understand what was going on around me. Staff treated me as if I was crazy and saw only the behavior that reinforced their belief system. I felt as if I was in a dream, another kind of reality or dimension, separated by some invisible barrier. I was in a place where only certain messages or interactions could pass through the barrier. None of the things I wanted to communicate could penetrate the barrier; only the mistakes, negatives, and nonaffirmations of me could get through.

The hospital experience fosters regression. You are there because you are perceived to be unable to see to your needs or because you are believed to be a threat to others. You cannot be trusted and must be monitored. How can such a negatively defined role make a person feel more adequate? I vowed not to regress. "I am not a child," I repeated to myself and anyone within earshot.

Only four months after I was admitted, lack of choice forced me to accept the only role that was available to me in this hospital drama: submissive patient. I said the right things and did nothing to draw attention to myself. Lacking the energy to do otherwise, my responses were "appropriate." I became self-protective, selfish, and interested only in meeting my own needs. Earlier my energy had centered on discharge, but now even those requests lacked force. I spoke little, responding only if required. When visitors came, I half listened, my requests focused on material items—cigarettes, money, food. My soul, my Èlan vital, had taken a sabbatical. An empty shell was left to deal with physical needs. In brief moments of clarity, I panicked at the thought of never having my vitality return.

Thin skin has been a mixed blessing for me. What helps me now as a therapist, I hated as a child. When practicing psychotherapy, I am respected for my ability to understand and empathize with feelings that go beyond what is consciously expressed. The child receives no reward for feeling the denied pain of others. As a therapist, I call up experiences from my past to connect with the experience of an *other.* Needs for acceptance, belonging, and recognition, so prominent during my childhood, are easy for me to recall.

I worked hard to get to where I am, and I give credit to myself and to the people who helped and supported me. But I have to believe that some other component was operating—luck or a spiritual, mystical quality. For years I thought I was alone and had defied the odds, slipping through the cracks and escaping the diagnosis that was promised to follow me all my life. I believed that I was an anomaly in my ability to leave my assigned mental patient role, to blend in, get married, be a father, and have a successful career as a psychologist. No more "symptoms," no more medication, no more therapy. Why were there not more people out there like me? To my delight I discovered my peers and found community. There are many of us who have walked through the fire. We who have survived are available to help our brothers and sisters develop their own unique maps for navigating not only their confusing and frightening internal struggles, but the even more damaging spirit-breaking treatments forced on them in unenlightened treatment facilities.

An Intensive Bottom-to-Top Training of Psychiatric Hospital Staff by Former Patients

At the start of the twenty-first century, we have witnessed first the steep growth and then the rapid decline of the number of publicly run state psychiatric hospitals. Yet despite the smaller number of people being confined to inpatient psychiatric facilities today, these institutions continue to be used as a last-resort safety net for the mental health system. Regardless of one's beliefs concerning the benefits or necessity of treating people in a psychiatric hospital, it is essential to determine what is harmful and what is helpful to people during their stays as inpatients and to implement practices that reflect this knowledge.

How to train all hospital staff to provide the best possible services to patients was the charge given to the designers of the New York State Office of Mental Health's (NYSOMH) *Core Curriculum: Direct Staff Training.* To accomplish this task, the following guidelines were established:

The core curriculum training would be a mandatory, three-day training event.
All ward staff would be trained together as a group and would include all
    workers who had any direct contact with inpatients: therapy aides, nurses,
    physicians, psychologists, social workers, housekeepers, administrative
    staff, and security.
Consumers/survivors/ex-patients (c/s/x) would participate fully in the devel-
    opment and implementation of the core curriculum.

In 1997 the NYSOMH initiated a two-year core curriculum training program for its nineteen state-operated psychiatric centers. The three-day training was divided into six modules:

Module A: Team Training, NYSOMH, and the Changing Nature of Mental Health Services
Module B: Working in a Changing Environment
Module C: Recovery and Mental Health
Module D: Selected Clinical Issues in Mental Health
Module E: Cultural Competence
Module F: Safe and Therapeutic Environment

This chapter cites the results gathered as of January 1, 1999, from exit questionnaires completed by 3,732 staff members and a sample of staff and inpatients from three facilities who completed both pre- and posttraining: a questionnaire, the Ward Atmosphere Scale, and the Work Environment Scale.[1]

As a c/s/x and a psychologist I participated in the planning, development, and implementation of all the modules. However, because of the innovative qualities of the recovery module, most significantly its reliance on c/s/x to develop and provide the training to staff, that module will be the central focus here.

Development of the Recovery Module

From the beginning, the NYSOMH recognized that expertise developed through the lived experience of persons who had been diagnosed and treated for major mental illness would be a valuable asset for staff training. NYSOMH commissioner James Stone solidified his office's commitment in his introduction to the first statewide train-the-trainer meeting by stating, "During your training you will have an opportunity to hear from individuals who use or have used the services we provide. In participating in this training as your trainers, service recipients are demonstrating the hope gained from new information showing many individuals with severe psychiatric disabilities are able to regain their lives and become productive members of our communities (Bassman, 1997)."

To develop the recovery module, c/s/x leaders across the state were surveyed and asked what they considered the most important elements in recovery. A review of published writings by c/s/x (Campbell and Schraiber, 1989; Chamberlin, 1997; Grobe, 1995; Hirsh and others, 1974; Susko, 1991) demonstrated a consistent emphasis on the same key themes identified by our survey. The following key themes were identified as instrumental to recovery and transformation:

There must be real choices. When people are forced to participate in programs and services not of their choosing, motivation suffers and passivity and learned helplessness develop.

Hope must be nurtured and cultivated.

People must be able to speak for themselves.

People want to be seen as a many-faceted whole person with a variety of strengths and weaknesses. They are individuals, not categories, labels or diagnoses.

Self-help, empowerment, and mutual support are important.

Services need to be provided in a respectful collaboration.

Communication must be two way.

Anger can be a positive force.

The next step was the development of a flexible guide for c/s/x trainers that would allow them to use their unique skills and experience, while also enabling them to cover the key concepts and themes. We had the themes and concepts that we wanted to convey, but wondered how we could get mental hospital staff to listen and learn from people whom they had seen only at their worst, when they were deemed to be so out of control that they needed to be in the strictly structured setting of a mental hospital. In addition, we wanted staff to get more than a few cold intellectual facts; we wanted them to be moved by what they saw and heard.

The solution became obvious: have people tell their stories of recovery. Based on their personal experience, they would talk about what was helpful and what was harmful. C/S/X trainers were encouraged to cover all of the key concepts and to illustrate them with anecdotes from their lives. Those who were unable to draw an example from their own life were encouraged to do a dramatic reading of another c/s/x's story that connected to their experience. People were encouraged to use art, music, games, or any other creative medium for making a point. One trainer decided to begin the training covered by a white sheet to demonstrate that you cannot get to know a person until you really see that person fully.

Another part of the recovery presentations focused on wants and needs. The audience was asked to call out the things they want and need to live a good life. After the exercise, a discussion ensued of the similarities of patients' wants and needs to those of staff (among them were personal goals, choice, social integration, relationships, constitutional and human rights, dignity and respect, health, a decent environment, security, personal satisfaction, and hope).

The three-hour presentation concluded with a discussion of people's beliefs about mental illness, different theories of mental illness, and some discussion of why people find psychiatric drugs problematic.

Recruiting and Training C/S/X Presenters for the Recovery Module

From the start we wanted to do all we could to make it possible for c/s/x to present in a safe, supportive environment where their participation would be growth enhancing and that its value would be reflected in adequate financial remuneration for their time and unique expertise. C/S/X would never be asked to present alone and were advised to present in groups of three for mutual support. Facilities staff were asked to have a room available, preferably with beverages and light refreshments, for presenters to relax and debrief with each other after presentations. A staff member at each facility was assigned to be the contact and support person should any unusual needs arise. Periodically presenters from different facilities met together to share their experiences of presenting, exchange helpful techniques of presenting, and network and support each other. Such all-day gatherings were centered around a discussion of questions like the following:

- What were some of the highlights of presenting the recovery module?
- How did staff respond to the training?
- Did you feel that the core curriculum staff were supportive of your efforts?
- What kind of supports did you use after presenting the recovery module?
- How did the training affect your own growth and development?
- What were some of the negative aspects for you during the recovery training? What would you have liked to have seen happen differently?
- What advice or suggestions would you give future c/s/x trainers?

Reactions of C/S/X Trainers to their Experiences as Presenters

Just about all of the c/s/x trainers were positive about their experiences of presenting their stories to staff. For many, this was an opportunity to find value and give meaning to their intense and often dehumanizing struggles. Following are examples of feedback from the c/s/x trainers that were shared during our group retreat:

- "Made people think. They seemed to look at things in a different light."
- "Doctors and social workers came up to presenters and cried."
- "Great; seeing oneself as equal to professionals."
- "Feel I have a lot to offer."
- "Brought back a lot of feelings I hadn't thought about."
- "Felt the depth of pain for me and my copresenters."
- "Self-esteem and confidence improved."
- "Speaking about personal experiences makes them less painful."
- "Breaking stigma by looking different than people think you will."
- "Learning that there is something more than what we have been taught."

Evaluation of the Impact of the Recovery Module

Overall findings indicated that the training was well received and viewed positively by approximately 80 percent of the staff. Many of the staff, including the veterans, commented that this was the best training they had ever attended.

The exit questionnaires rated the recovery module highest of the six modules in having the most effect on change. More than half of the staff thought that the recovery training would result in the following improvements:

- Greater staff acceptance of patients' speaking up for their rights.
- A substantial improvement in the respect given to patient privacy.
- See people as individuals rather than just as a diagnosis or a mental patient.
- A substantial effect on ward environment and procedures to enhance recovery.
- Improvement in patients' being able to express their feelings without getting into trouble.
- Patients are being allowed to tell their whole story before staff makes up their mind.

The quarterly reports completed by facility directors confirmed that the recovery module contained the most powerful message. The reports indicated that staff were making positive changes in their relationships to patients, and in committee meetings they were paying more attention to issues of patient respect and privacy. Staff were more willing to accept patient input as relevant and see the value of patients' expressing their concerns.

Results of the more intensive evaluations conducted at three selected facilities confirmed the positive impact of the recovery module. Pre- and posttraining comparisons that staff made indicated statistically significant improvement in the following areas:

- A significant increase in staff's belief that what recipients say should make a difference in treatment
- A significant increase in staff's willingness to attempt to make improvements on the ward in order to enhance recovery possibilities
- A significant increase in staff's belief that people can recover, get out of the hospital, and never come back

Patients residing on the hospital wards completed questionnaires before staff participated in the training and responded again to those questions twelve to fifteen weeks after staff training was completed. Three questions showed statistically significant improvement from the patients' perspectives:

- Staff would allow them freer expression without their getting into trouble.
- Staff saw patients more as individuals and not just as a mental health patient or diagnosis.

- More patients wanted to increase the frequency of their interaction with staff.

Puncturing Stereotypes: Seeing Real People

How well can we understand someone else's internal experience? The old adage said that you do not have to be a woman who has given birth to be qualified to deliver a baby. But can someone who has not gone through the labor of birthing a baby truly comprehend the magnitude of this process? When a woman talks with another woman about their labor and birthing experiences, there is an immediate understanding and bonding. Can there be empathy without having had a commonality of experience? Of course, empathic understanding is not an all-or-nothing, you-have-it-or-you-do-not proposition. Yet it is difficult to deny that all other things being equal, those who have been through an experience will have a better understanding of a similar experience than those who have not.

The absence of genuine empathy in the treatment of people diagnosed with serious mental illness arises from a long history of fear, misunderstanding, and exclusion. Treatments have often been illogical, nonsensical, and downright cruel. Lobotomies, cold packs, insulin comas, physical beatings, and other forms of torture have been foisted on people as if they were objects that could not think, feel, or express their own wants and needs. Such magical thinking about what constitutes effective treatment was considered science, while the attribution of magical thinking to a potential patient is a key element in the diagnosis of schizophrenia. Often unproven assumptions about mental illness are regarded as facts and strung together to make theories that treatment teams use to ignore or make short shrift of what people say is going on within themselves

How do those who have never been a patient in a mental hospital develop the understanding that is helpful in treating people who have experienced the kinds of thinking, feelings, and behavior that would get them committed to a mental hospital? Through personal experience, c/s/x know the importance of having staff listen and try to understand and accept the validity of their experiences. After a person is hospitalized, it is easy and natural for him or her to spiral downward. The unfamiliar surroundings, the uncertainty as to what will happen next, the probing questions, and the cold and impersonal interactions with staff intensify fear and panic. Many c/s/x are brought to the hospital at night and processed through procedures with no explanation or hint of warmth or human contact.

If someone had sat and talked with us, told us what to expect the next day, would there have been more cooperation? Could I have avoided the forced drugging and disorientation? Would I have been able to avoid seclusion and restraint and the hostile adversarial reactions I felt toward staff?

Staff of inpatient psychiatric hospitals rarely have the opportunity to see people who have recovered and have gone on with their lives. They see people at their worst, and in artificial micromanaged settings. They do not get the chance to benefit from learning how much value people place on the small acts of kindness and respect that are shown to them. Nor do they learn of the negative impact of thoughtless words and deeds.

Repeatedly staff members approached c/s/x after their presentations to thank them for letting them know that patients really appreciated it when they were related to in a warm and personal way. Particularly effective was the presentation of one c/s/x who told about lying immobile on her bed in the ward staring at the ceiling. She was unable to look at anyone or respond in any way. Yet she fondly remembers one nurse who daily came into the room and ask her if she wanted a blanket or wanted the light turned on or off. And although she did not respond, she has always remembered that nurse's kindness and cites it as an uplifting human connection that helped her recover. Staff were extremely interested and surprised to find out that even people who looked completely unresponsive remained aware, and no matter how disoriented they seemed, they did not lose all of their capabilities.

Mental health therapy aides were especially pleased to learn that so many people were grateful for the very small acts of kindness extended to them. Many c/s/x cited those acts of caring, interest, and respectful listening as the initial building block of their recovery. The feeling that someone believed in them and thought that they could do better cultivated hope.

Another powerful anecdote was told by a c/s/x who was working in a psychiatric hospital as a peer advocate after her own discharge. Her story demonstrated the negative impact of invalidating a person's feelings. She was listening to a woman angrily complain to her about the failure of her advocacy efforts to get what was requested. Since these advocacy efforts were ineffective, she knew that the patient's complaints were justified, and she was willing to listen to her express her disappointment. At that time, a psychiatrist was on the ward, and knowing both the advocate and the patient, he decided to intervene. He faced the advocate and with his back to the patient said condescendingly, "You know some people need to learn that you never get what you want if you get angry at people who are trying to help you." And then he walked away. Immediately this patient began hallucinating and responding to her inner voices, whereas before, although she was angry, she had rationally expressed her displeasure. Now, after being treated as if she was not there by a powerful doctor who had control of her future, she was forced to suppress her feelings and withdraw into her mental patient role. Communication had ended between her and her advocate.

Conclusion

Those of us who have been through cataclysmic, life-altering experiences are able to provide empathic understanding and serve as models to inspire hope. The capacity to offer meaningful help is not limited to the consumer/survivor/ex-patient. The examined life is entered into in many ways. Any form of illness or violation of what we have come to expect our minds and bodies to be has the potential to alter the way we construe our experiences and attempt to integrate them into meaningful narratives.

As observers, we are always outside and therefore can only see, measure, and evaluate a particular person through the lens of the most recent snapshot photo that we are encountering now. You are not able to know the unique personal history that an individual construes for himself or herself or predict that person's future. However, your influence on a person's vision of his past and future can open possibilities in the present.

Note

1. See *Core Curriculum Final Evaluation Report,* Bruce Way & Barbara Stone, NYSOMH Bureau of Performance Measurement, 44 Holland Ave., Albany, NY 12229, December 1, 1999.

References

Bassman, R. "The Mental Health System: Experiences from Both Sides of the Locked Doors." *Professional Psychology: Research and Practice,* 1997, 28(3), 238–242.

Campbell, J., and Schraiber, R. *The Well-Being Project: Mental Health Clients Speak for Themselves.* Sacramento: California Department of Mental Health, 1989.

Chamberlin, J. "Confessions of a Non-Compliant Patient." *National Empowerment Center Newsletter,* Summer/Fall 1997, 9, 13.

Grobe, J. (ed.). *Beyond Bedlam: Contemporary Women Psychiatric Survivors Speak Out.* Chicago: Third Side Press, 1995.

Hirsh, S., and others (eds.). *Madness Network News Reader.* San Francisco: Glide Publications, 1974.

Susko, M. (ed.). *Cry of the Invisible: Writings from the Homeless and Survivors of Psychiatric Hospitals.* Baltimore, Md.: Conservatory Press, 1991.

Way, B., and Stone, B. (1999). *Core Curriculum Final Evaluation Report.* Albany, N.Y.: New York State Office of Mental Health, 1999.

RONALD BASSMAN is coordinator of self-help and empowerment projects for the New York State Office of Mental Health in Albany, New York, and is president of the National Association for Rights Protection and Advocacy.

*A clinical psychologist reveals how a breakthrough, trans-
formational experience was perceived as a schizophrenic
breakdown and led to his being placed on the back ward
of a VA psychiatric hospital.*

My Transforming Peak Experience Was Diagnosed as Paranoid Schizophrenia

Al Siebert

Soon after I finished my doctoral program in clinical psychology at the University of Michigan in 1965, I went through a powerful transformation. Once started, the process swept me along with its own energy. Synchronicity with new events and incidents kept it going week after week. I experienced breakthrough insights that kept coming and coming. I allowed myself to experience forbidden thoughts and feelings that freed my mind from false and erroneous beliefs in psychiatry and clinical psychology.

During this time I moved to Topeka, Kansas, to start a two-year post-doctoral fellowship in clinical psychology at the Menninger Foundation. The fellowship was a significant honor. Out of dozens of applicants from all over the world, I was one of only three selected.

When a psychologist and a psychiatrist at Menninger's asked me what I was thinking, they were not good listeners. They declared me mentally ill and canceled my fellowship. They had me placed on the back ward of the local Veterans Administration hospital diagnosed with "acute paranoid schizophrenia." They insisted that I was deeply disturbed and needed years of treatment. Four weeks later, I signed out "Against Medical Advice" and returned home to begin applying my new ways of seeing, thinking, and feeling.

In the thirty-five years since then, I've enjoyed a very fulfilling life—both personally and professionally. By telling my story now, I hope to show that someone declared to be paranoid schizophrenic may be much different from what psychiatrists typically report. For too many decades, psychiatrists have been allowed to present their explanation of a mental patient and the patient's side as well. This situation is equivalent to allowing a plaintiff's attorney to present the defendant's case while barring the defendant from the courtroom.

The Seeds of Transformation

In March 1965, I'd finished all my coursework in the clinical psychology program at the University of Michigan, and was about to start my dissertation research. My supervisor at the Neuropsychiatric Institute at the University of Michigan hospital, where I worked half time as a staff psychologist, called me into his office one afternoon. He said he wanted me to apply for a two-year postdoctoral fellowship at the Menninger Foundation. I had no interest in doing postdoctoral work, but he insisted, so I sent in an application.

A week later, Martin Mayman, director of psychology training at Menninger's, telephoned and invited me to Topeka for two days of interviews. Not expecting to get the fellowship, I treated the trip like a paid visit to the capital of psychiatry. I stayed relaxed and enjoyed meeting all the psychologists on my interview schedule. Several weeks after my interviews, Mayman telephoned me and said I'd been selected to be one of the three Fellows chosen to start in September.

I completed my dissertation and passed my oral defense in June. Although I began working full time as a psychologist at NPI, I now had more free time than I was accustomed to. I began to reflect on what I'd learned in graduate school. I thought about the Menninger program and liked that it encouraged Fellows to question clinical assumptions.

I wrote a list of questions I was curious about. I found myself wondering why most efforts to make the world better center on trying to get other people to change.

I read *Atlas Shrugged,* by Ayn Rand, and was fascinated with her portrayals of ways that people act in selfish ways while denying their selfish motives. At NPI I witnessed a psychiatric resident insisting to a resistant patient, "I'm doing this for your own good." I speculated that people who force unwanted help onto others are subconsciously trying to build up their self-esteem.

I watched a resident insisting and then shouting at a patient that he had to accept that he was mentally ill. The patient kept shouting back that he wasn't.

Learning that such actions take place behind closed doors in psychiatrists' offices surprised me. I'd read hundreds of articles and books about psychotherapy research, but none of them addressed whether or not patients were told they must believe that they are mentally ill. I realized that research reports about psychiatric treatment are badly flawed because they are silent about this significant variable.

I meditated a lot and went for long walks by myself. I was seeing and discovering much about the actual practice of psychiatry that was not taught in my courses.

I saw that forcing unwanted help on others seems to be a way to subconsciously build up one's own self-esteem. I wondered how I could identify hidden selfish motives in myself, and take my need for esteem away from the control of others. Could I do that by allowing myself to have high self-esteem? Creative experimentation led me to conclude that the highest possible statement of self-esteem would be, "As far as I am concerned, I am the most valuable person who will ever exist." This would be a private feeling that would leave others free to have the same feeling. For me, this phrase would not be a comparative term such as "the best" or "better than."

It occurred to me that the need for high esteem might be why people claim to be Jesus, Cleopatra, Napoleon, the Virgin Mary, or such. My hypothesis was that if a person's self-esteem had been driven down, there might be a subconscious, homeostatic mechanism that tries to rescue it. I wondered how I could test my hypothesis.

Experimental Interview. A few days later at NPI, we heard at morning rounds that an eighteen-year-old woman had been brought in by her parents during the weekend. The psychiatric resident in charge of the patient said, "The parents told us that Molly claims God talked to her. My provisional diagnosis is that she is a paranoid schizophrenic. She is very withdrawn. She won't talk to me or the nurses."

Each morning we heard that Molly would not talk to anyone. She refused to go to recreational therapy, occupational therapy, or any ward activities. She stopped talking to her doctor. After two weeks of such reports, the senior supervising psychiatrist said to the resident, "This patient is not responding to our treatment milieu. She is so severely withdrawn you should start the paperwork to have her committed to Ypsilanti State Hospital."

Most of the staff nodded in agreement. One of the staff psychiatrists said, "Molly is so severely paranoid schizophrenic she will probably spend the rest of her life in the state hospital."

I saw that this might be a chance to test out some of my hypotheses. Since Molly was headed for a lifetime on the back wards, I didn't think I could do any harm. I obtained permission from the resident to interview Molly and do a few psychological tests before she was transferred. Then I arranged with the head nurse on the locked ward to interview Molly in the ward dining room the next morning.

That night I mentally prepared myself for the next day. Professor Jim McConnell was my adviser my first two years in graduate school. He constantly challenged me to look at behaviors and their consequences. With this in mind, I developed four questions to use as guidelines:

- What would happen if I just listened to her and don't allow my mind to put any psychiatric labels on her?
- What would happen if I talked to her believing that she could turn out to be my best friend?

- What would happen if I accepted everything she reports about herself as being the truth?
- What would happen if I questioned her to find out if there's a link between her self-esteem, the workings of her mind, and the way that others have been treating her?

During my interview with Molly the next day, she told me about the events that led up to her being in the hospital. She was an only child. She wanted her parents' love, but they didn't give her much. Only once in a while. Just enough to give her hope she could get more.

She would come home from high school and volunteer to help with the housework, the cooking, and the dishes. But her mother rarely showed any appreciation. Her father had been a musician, so she took up the clarinet in high school. She thought this would please him. Her senior year she was chosen to be first chair in the high school orchestra.

"I was excited," she said. "I believed my father would be proud of me. When he came home that night I told him. But he got angry. He picked up my clarinet and smashed it across the kitchen table. He yelled at me, 'You'll never amount to anything.'"

"How did you feel after that?"

"Awful. I cried and cried. I knew my parents didn't love me."

"What happened after you graduated from high school?"

"I spent the summer with my boyfriend. At the end of summer I went to nursing school and he went to a university in a different city."

"Why did you choose nursing?"

"I thought the patients would like me for all the nice things I would do for them."

"What was nursing school like for you?"

"I kept to myself. I didn't make friends with other student nurses except for one. We had to study a lot. The third term I got my first clinical assignment. I was really looking forward to it." Molly looked down.

"What happened?" I asked.

"The two women in my room criticized me." Molly's face twisted in pain. "I couldn't do anything right for them."

"How did you feel when that happened?"

"Like the world was falling in. It was horrible." She dropped her head. "I ran away from school. I took a bus to where my boyfriend was at college. He came and met me at the bus station. We went to a coffee shop to talk. I said I wanted to come and live with him, but he said he wanted to date other girls. He said we could still be friends, but I should go home and write to him."

"How did you feel after that?"

"Awful lonely."

"What did you do?"

"I left school and went back home."

"How did your parents feel about that?"

"They didn't want me there."

"And you felt. . . ."

"Lonely. I stayed in my room most the time."

"So your dad and mom didn't love you. The patients were critical. They didn't like you. Your boyfriend just wanted to be friends. Your parents didn't want you to come back to live with them."

"Yes, there didn't seem to be anyone in the whole world who cared for me at all."

"What an awful feeling. And then God spoke to you."

"Yes," she said in a soft voice.

"How did you feel after God gave you the good news?"

Molly looked up with a warm inner radiance and smiled. "I felt like the most special person in the whole world."

"That's a nice feeling, isn't it?"

"Yes, it is."

Two days later, I went up to the locked ward to pick up a patient scheduled for testing. When Molly saw me, she walked up to me and said, "I've been thinking about what we talked about. I've been wondering. Do you think I imagined God's voice to make myself feel better?"

I was amazed. I didn't intend to do therapy, but she seemed to see the connection.

"Perhaps," I said, shrugging and smiling.

At rounds during the next week, we heard that Molly was talking to people, participating in ward activities, dressing better, and wearing makeup. The plan to commit her was postponed. The supervising psychiatrist said, "This may be a case of spontaneous remission. You can never predict when it will happen."

It fascinated me that a patient they couldn't cure suddenly got better, and they viewed the recovery as happening all by itself. No one was curious or asked questions. During my last week at NPI, I was pleased to hear Molly's doctor announce at rounds that Molly seemed to be fully recovered and had been transferred to the open ward.

My wife was upset with my preoccupied state. She pleaded with me to talk about what I was thinking. When I told her about my hypothesis about self-esteem and about Molly, she became so distressed she went to church to talk to a priest.

Stress Reactions in the Minds of Beholders. Martin Mayman left Menninger's during the summer. Shortly after my wife and I arrived in Topeka and rented an apartment, the acting director telephoned and asked me to meet with him. He showed me my office and asked if I felt I could handle the pressures of the program. I assured him that I could. Several days later, he telephoned me again and said that my wife was going to start into psychotherapy. He said he wanted me to go with her for an interview with a psychiatrist at the outpatient clinic. I felt suspicious, but agreed.

At the clinic the receptionist sent both of us upstairs to see the psychiatrist. After several minutes of superficial talk, he said, "Mrs. Siebert, will you please go down to the waiting room? I want to speak to Dr. Siebert privately."

This confirmed my suspicion. A spouse is *never* interviewed first before their partner starts therapy. After she left, he said, "We would like some help from you. What do you think is upsetting your wife?"

I paused, knowing that I was at a choice point in my life. I asked myself, "Should I be honest with him or should I only tell him what I think he can handle?" I decided that if I had to be deceptive to keep the fellowship, then it wasn't worth having. I said, "It could be some of my ideas."

"Tell me about some of these ideas," he said.

I laid it all out for him. I described my speculations about why an underlying need for self-esteem motivates people to force unwanted help onto others and about two defense mechanisms Freud hadn't seen. I told him about my interview with Molly, about my experiment with a statement of high self-esteem, and a double-bind that psychiatrists put a patient in when they say, "you must accept into your mind the thought that you are mentally ill because you believe people are trying to force thoughts into your mind."

"I've tried to explain all this to my wife," I said, "but she can't handle it."

"She is disturbed and depressed," he said. "What are your feelings about her calling us up and asking for this consultation?"

"I appreciate the fact that she saved me a lot of time. I had been wondering how to bring these ideas to the attention of the staff."

His face showed surprise. "You wanted us to know about your ideas?"

"Of course. I figured that the best place to begin a new breakthrough in the field of mental health was from the leading psychiatric facility in the world."

The psychiatrist had the receptionist send my wife back in. After she seated herself, he said, "You were right. Mrs. Siebert. He is mentally ill."

"What!" I blurted out. I was halfway expecting it, but wanted so much for him to understand my thinking that his words came as a shock.

"You are the one who is mentally ill, Dr. Siebert, not your wife."

When I protested that my ideas made sense, he said, "I am not going to argue. You *are* mentally ill and you need to be in an institution."

On the way home, my wife confessed that the acting director called me because she had telephoned him. She said that the priest in Ann Arbor had advised her to contact psychologists and psychiatrists who knew me and ask them to get help for me.

The next morning, the acting director telephoned and told me to come to his office. When I arrived, he said, "We have decided that to protect our program, we have to let you go. We cannot trust you with our patients. How do you feel about that?"

"I believe that you have the right and the responsibility to do what you think is best for your program," I said. "I'll go figure out another way to present my ideas to psychiatrists."

"We don't want you to do that," he said. "You need to stay here and go into the hospital. You are quite mentally ill."

"My ideas make sense if you'd listen. Look, I've been—"

He shook his head to stop me. "The psychiatrist at the clinic went into that with you yesterday, and he decided that these ideas are symptoms of illness. You need to be in an institution."

"What I need is to be left alone. Throughout all this my only request is for people to get off my back."

"But we don't want you to do anything that might ruin your career. You do seem to have some good skills."

"I must go into a mental hospital in order to *not* have my career ruined?"

"Yes," he said. "You are mentally ill and need long-term psychotherapy."

"And you're only doing this for my own good?"

"Yes."

"No selfish reasons motivate you?"

"Assuredly not."

On Saturday morning, the clinic psychiatrist telephoned me. "You are very sick, Dr. Siebert," he said. "You need to go into a hospital." He said he knew I was a military veteran and that there was an excellent Veterans Administration psychiatric hospital in Topeka. "The director of the hospital is a friend of mine," he said. "He has authorized your immediate admission. If I drive over and pick you up, will you let me take you over?"

Another choice point. I wondered if I should take off or go along with them. Three months of mental and emotional turmoil had me feeling tired and wrung out. I was in a new city with no one who knew me well. I knew how easy it was for psychiatrists to have someone involuntarily committed. I decided that if I went in voluntarily, it would be much easier to get out later. I said, "OK."

Thirty minutes later, as we were driving to the hospital, he said, "You have made a wise decision. You will be better off now." He drove with an artificial smile frozen on his face. His face glistened with sweat. His hands gripped the wheel so tightly his knuckles were white.

"You know," I said, "this will be an interesting experience for me. Any time I go into a new situation I learn a great deal from it. This should prove to be the same. I know I'll learn a lot."

A look of pity swept over his face as he glanced at me. He seemed to be thinking, "You poor deluded soul. So out of contact with reality you are happy and optimistic about your plight."

"I'm disappointed," I said, "that we didn't have longer to talk. I didn't have a good chance to tell you all about my ideas."

"Would you like to tell me more?"

"Yes. No one has given me a full chance yet. Would you be willing to come over and talk with me?"

He turned and smiled at me. "Yes, I'd like that."

I didn't believe him. He was doing what psychiatrists commonly do. Lies and deceptions are OK if it will get the person locked up without force. I'd like to see an article in a psychiatric journal justifying their habit of lying to people that they think are mentally ill. It's like trying to open a savings account by writing a bad check.

My Accelerated Postdoctoral Education. I spent Saturday and Sunday on a well-run ward. On Monday I was taken to a different ward. I laughed when I saw that I'd been transferred to the back ward with the most chronic, deteriorated, heavily medicated patients in the hospital. The efforts to make me accept that their perception of me was more accurate than my own were too transparent.

During the next four weeks I learned more about psychiatry from the accelerated postdoctoral education that the Menninger people arranged for me than I would have from two years in their formal program.

I stayed in the hospital until they held my admission case conference. The way the Menninger people reacted to my breakthrough insights was so bizarre, I anticipated that in future years they might try to deny what they did. I knew that staying in the hospital until my case conference was held would ensure that my hospitalization would be documented in the permanent medical records of the VA system.

My case conference was held about four weeks after my admission. After the conference I "eloped" from the hospital. The next day I telephoned the ward psychiatrist and arranged with him to go back and sign an "Against Medical Advice" discharge form in exchange for my wallet, keys, and watch.

Thirty-Five Years Later

My months-long, transformational experience was the best thing that ever happened to me. What I went through closely matched Maslow's description of self-actualizing peak experiences. I was in state of high consciousness knowing that everything was happening exactly as it should. I felt joyously disillusioned in ways that freed my mind. Once I saw that the perception of mental illness is mostly a delusion in the mind of the beholder, everything fell into place.

My experience taught me that the so-called mental health profession is really a mental illness profession that has little understanding of mental health. After I returned home, I decided to focus my efforts on researching and teaching about the inner nature of highly resilient survivors (Siebert, 1996).

When I run across my old VA hospital record, I have mixed feelings. I chuckle when I see the diagnosis "Schizophrenic reaction, paranoid type, acute," and "Discharged AMA." At the same time, I feel sorrow for people diagnosed as schizophrenic who don't know how to survive "help" forced on them that is frequently more harmful than beneficial.

My contempt for psychiatrists who misrepresent what is known about schizophrenia to the public has not abated (Siebert, 1999). Many psychiatrists, for example, are currently declaring that schizophrenia is "a brain disease like Alzheimer's, Parkinson's, and multiple sclerosis" (Farnsworth, 1998). They say this even though decades of research have established that from 20 percent to 30 percent of the people who go through a "schizophrenic" period fully and completely recover from the condition and can do so with no medications.

There are many such examples that something is seriously wrong with psychiatry. I believe that no significant progress in treatment outcomes with "mental illnesses" will occur until research explores the cognitive processes, motives, and personalities of people in the "mental health" field (Siebert, 2000). For the sake of thousands of so-called schizophrenic patients who have been told that they have an incurable brain disease and are forced to take neurologically harmful medications, I hope it happens soon.

References

Farnsworth, E. "Unstable Minds." Transcript of Jim Lehrer's *NewsHour* on-line. Available at: http://www.pbs.org/newshour/home.html. Past programs file, July 27, 1998.

Siebert, A. *The Survivor Personality.* New York: Berkley/Perigee Books, 1996.

Siebert, A. "Brain Disease Hypothesis for Schizophrenia Disconfirmed by All Evidence." *Journal of Ethical Human Sciences and Services,* 1999, *1* (2), 179–189.

Siebert, A. "How Non-Diagnostic Listening Led to a Rapid 'Recovery' from Paranoid Schizophrenia: What Is Wrong with Psychiatry?" *Journal of Humanistic Psychology,* 2000, *40* (1), 34–58.

AL SIEBERT is with the Center for Professional Development at Portland State University. He is host of the Web sites "successful schizophrenia" (www.webcom.com/thrive/schizo/) and "THRIVEnet.com" (www.thrivenet.com).

INDEX

Back Issue/Subscription Order Form

Copy or detach and send to:
Jossey-Bass, 350 Sansome Street, San Francisco CA 94104-1342

Call or fax toll free!
Phone 888-378-2537 6AM-5PM PST; Fax 800-605-2665

Back issues: Please send me the following issues at $25 each.
(Important: please include series initials and issue number, such as MHS90.)

1. MHS   _____

_____

$ _____ Total for single issues

$ _____ Shipping charges (for single issues **only;** subscriptions are exempt
from shipping charges): Up to $30, add $5^{50} • $30^{01}–$50, add $6^{50}
$50^{01}–$75, add $8 • $75^{01}–$100, add $10 • $100^{01}–$150, add $12
Over $150, call for shipping charge

Subscriptions   Please ❏ start   ❏ renew my subscription to *New Directions for
Mental Health Services* for the year ____ at the following rate:

U.S.:	❏ Individual $66	❏ Institutional $121
Canada:	❏ Individual $66	❏ Institutional $161
All others:	❏ Individual $90	❏ Institutional $195

$ _____ Total single issues and subscriptions (Add appropriate sales tax for
your state for single issue orders. No sales tax for U.S. subscriptions.
Canadian residents, add GST for subscriptions.)

❏ Payment enclosed (U.S. check or money order only)
❏ VISA, MC, AmEx, Discover Card #_____ Exp. date_____

Signature _____ Day phone _____
❏ Bill me (U.S. institutional orders only. Purchase order required.)
Purchase order #_____

Federal Tax ID 135593032   GST 89102-8052

Name _____

Address _____

_____

Phone_____ E-mail _____

For more information about Jossey-Bass, visit our Web site at:
www.josseybass.com   **PRIORITY CODE = ND1**

OTHER TITLES AVAILABLE IN THE NEW DIRECTIONS FOR MENTAL HEALTH
SERVICES SERIES
H. Richard Lamb, Editor-in-Chief